MEGAN STEPHENS

with Jane Smith

BOUGHT & SOLD

A 14-year-old British girl trafficked
for sex by the man she loved

HarperElement
An imprint of HarperCollins*Publishers*
1 London Bridge Street
London SE1 9GF

www.harpercollins.co.uk

First published by HarperElement 2015

1 3 5 7 9 10 8 6 4 2

A catalogue record of this book is
available from the British Library

PB ISBN 978-0-00-759407-8
EB ISBN 978-0-00-759408-5

Printed and bound in the United States
of America by RR Donnelley

Find out more about HarperCollins and the environment at
www.harpercollins.co.uk/green

Acknowledgements

I would like to express my gratitude to the many people who have supported and stuck by me throughout my recovery process.

First, I would like to give special thanks to John and Anthony for giving me the strength to carry on through life and for showing me that men are not all the same.

I would also like to thank the girls in recovery I have met along the way for their inspiration and encouragement to keep going, my grandparents for their gentle and loving hearts, and all the other amazing people who have given me hope and become my friends.

And thank you to my mum for all your support and love, especially during recent times. I love you so much.

Foreword

by Sophie Hayes*

I was pleased to be asked to write a foreword to Megan's deeply moving story. Then I thought about it a bit more and began to get anxious: it felt like a big responsibility to introduce something so personal and so incredibly important to Megan. I needn't have worried though. As soon as I read the manuscript of her amazing book *Bought and Sold*, I realised that Megan can speak for herself and that what I was really being asked to do was give my

---

* Sophie Hayes is the author of *Trafficked*, the *Sunday Times* number one bestselling memoir of 2012. After the publication of her book, Sophie set up the Sophie Hayes Foundation (www.sophiehayesfoundation.org), a charity that works tirelessly to raise awareness of human trafficking and provide support for its victims. In October 2014 she was awarded the Courage in Justice Award from the Crown Prosecution Association for the demonstration of bravery, inspiration and resilience in the face of adversity.

support to another survivor of sex trafficking. And as supporting survivors of human trafficking is a cause that's very close to my heart, I would like to add my voice to Megan's and reiterate a couple of the points she raises in her book.

One of the aspects of Megan's story that particularly struck me – apart from her bravery and the brutality of the treatment she endured for so long – was her explanation of the psychological fear that prevented her from trying to escape, even when she apparently had opportunities to do so.

Being paralysed by fear and by the belief that, in some way, you deserve the terrible things that are being done to you are common themes among people who've been trafficked for sex. I know it's an aspect that some people find impossible to understand. Perhaps I wouldn't have understood it either, before it happened to me.

The truth is that, although all human traffickers are ruthless criminals, most of them aren't stupid, and it isn't purely by chance that they choose victims who are likely to be compliant – and very frightened – in response to physical violence and psychological bullying. If reading Megan's story makes a few more people understand that, she will have done a great service to other victims and survivors of trafficking.

It wasn't very long ago that no one talked openly about child or domestic abuse. Then a few extraordinarily brave people told their stories and, gradually, we started to gain a better understanding of the true extent of these crimes and of the devastating effects they have on their victims. Now, we need to do the same thing in relation to human trafficking. By raising awareness of an appalling crime that can affect anyone, male or female, of any age, nationality, intellectual ability or social background, Megan's book may actually save lives.

At the Sophie Hayes Foundation, we've recently set up a Survivors' Network to enable young women like Megan to meet other women who've had similar experiences and who share their sense of isolation, guilt and loneliness. For some of our 'survivors', it's the first time they've been able to talk openly about their experiences to people they can trust. I've been touched and very impressed to witness the support they give each other; it's a privilege to watch them evolve and grow into the people they were always meant to be. One of the women in the Survivors' Network writes amazing poems, another is a talented artist, some have already been to college and others are about to start.

You don't ever 'get over' the experience of being trafficked: you never forget the physical assaults or the fear or the terrible, all-enveloping feeling of being alone. But, like Megan, you can refuse to be crushed by it or to allow your life to be defined by the horrific things that have happened to you.

When you have read Megan's story, you may still believe that you would never allow yourself to be coerced, intimidated and frightened into becoming a victim of human trafficking. But I hope that you will have some understanding of the reasons why many millions of people do become victims of it.

Preface

Every day for six years of my life I was afraid. It was during those years, when I was learning to live with fear, that I realised you never really know how you'll react in any situation that's beyond your normal experience. You might think you know what you would do, but you don't. In fact, there are a lot of things I probably wouldn't ever have known – about myself and about what other people are capable of – if I hadn't gone to Greece with my mum when I was 14 and fallen in love.

Looking back on it now, it's difficult to know whether what I felt for Jak was real love: all your emotions are intense when you're 14. But I certainly *thought* I loved him, and that he loved me. It's the only possible explanation of why – long past the point at which caring about him had become illogical and ridiculous – I missed what might have been my chance to escape. I don't have any feelings for him now, of course, and I've finally accepted the fact that he didn't ever love me.

I hope that when you've read my story, you'll understand why I won't ever identify the man I've called Jak, why I've changed the names of everyone in it and why I'm so afraid of the fear coming back.

My lack of courage makes me feel very guilty, not least because I know that there are other girls who've been forced into prostitution by the same human traffickers who tricked and controlled me. I don't have to try to imagine how miserable and frightened those girls are. I know how they feel as they fall asleep every night wishing the morning won't come so that they won't have to live through another day of violence, humiliation and aching loneliness. I felt that way myself almost every day for six years. Now, five years later, I still have nightmares, and I still sometimes forget how not to be afraid.

What happened to me in Greece stripped away the last remnants of my self-esteem. And when you think you're worthless, it's difficult to believe that *anyone* could love you. But I know my mum loves me and before I tell my story I just want to say that I love her too.

Perhaps things would have turned out differently if Mum had insisted on intervening more forcefully when I made my first really bad decision in Greece. The problem was that she didn't have any more idea than I did that there are actually people in the world who buy and sell human beings. So she believed me when I told her I was happy. She put the photographs I sent her up on the wall in the bar where she works, and she didn't suspect for a single moment that I was lying to her.

There are lots of incidents in my story that will make you wonder how anyone could be as stupid as I was. It's something I still don't really understand myself, except that I was very young and naïve when I fell in love with Jak. Perhaps that was at least part of the reason why I suspended what little commonsense I had and simply accepted everything he told me. And if I didn't realise what was happening, I certainly can't blame my mum for not realising it either.

Something else I didn't know until recently is that there are estimated to be more than *20 million* victims of forced labour – including victims of human trafficking for labour and sexual exploitation – throughout the world. That means that there are more than 20 million men, women and children whose lives have been stolen, who've been separated from their families and friends, and who are being forced to work incredibly long hours, often in appalling conditions. A significant number of those people will have been tricked, as I was, by someone they believed loved them or by the promise of legitimate work. I wouldn't for one moment blame any of them for what's happened to them. So I know I shouldn't blame myself, entirely, for what happened to me, although I still find it difficult not to.

I realise that by telling my story I'm exposing myself to the judgement of other people, some of whom won't be as understanding as I might hope. But if reading it makes just one person think twice before trusting someone they shouldn't trust, and as a consequence they don't take a step they'll regret for the rest of their lives, I'll feel that something positive has come out of it all.

Chapter 1

I was 14 when I went to Greece with my mum. At first, that seemed to be the obvious place to start my story. But when I really began to think about it, I realised it started much earlier than that, when I was just a little girl. Revisiting my childhood has helped me to understand why I later acted and reacted in some of the ways I did.

I was almost 12 years old when I began to develop from 'child with problems' into 'problem child'. Even at that young age, I already had a tightly coiled ball of anger inside me that sometimes erupted into bad behaviour. I wasn't ever violent; I was just argumentative and determined to do whatever daft, ill-advised thing I had set my mind on. Although I've always loved them both fiercely, I used to argue endlessly with my sister, and I would backchat my mum too, in the loudly defiant way some teenagers do. Then, at almost 12, I started wagging school and running away from home.

I feel sorry for Mum when I think about it now. It must have all been rather a shock for her, particularly as I had been quite a well-behaved, academically able little girl before then. I know she found it really difficult to deal with the new me, at a time when she had enough problems of her own.

I was four when my mum and dad split up. My earliest bad memory is of the day Dad left. I was sitting at the top of the stairs in our house, sobbing. I used to remember that day and think I was crying because I had a terrible stomach ache, until I realised that I get terrible stomach aches whenever I'm frightened or upset. So I think the tears – and the stomach ache – were because Dad was leaving.

When he came out of the living room into the hallway, I called down to him, 'Please, Dad, don't go.' When he stopped and looked up at me, I held my breath for a moment because I thought he might not be going to leave after all. But then he waved and walked out of the front door.

I adored my dad and in some ways I never get over his leaving. But I've got lots of good memories of my stepdad, John, who came to live with us not long after Dad left. I used to love school when I was young and one of the things I really liked about John was the way he always talked to me about whatever it was I was learning and then helped me with my homework. He was tidy too, unlike Dad, and the house was always clean and nice to live in when he was there.

We lived in a good area of town at that time. Mum had made sure of that. She said she wanted my sister and me to have more opportunities and a better life than she had had, which is also why she insisted on us always speaking and behaving 'properly'.

Dad had not moved very far away when he left – just to the other side of town – and some weekends my sister and I would go to stay with him. Mum told me later that he had started drinking and taking drugs before they split up. I didn't know about the drugs as a child, but I think I *was* aware that he drank, or, at least, I was aware of the consequences of his drinking, because of the sometimes scary way he behaved when he was drunk.

Whenever my sister and I went to stay with him, Mum would give him money so that he could look after us. But he must have spent it on alcohol, because we would go home on Sunday nights with tangled hair and dirty clothes, feeling ravenously hungry. It didn't make any difference to the way I felt about Dad though: I still adored him, and I would scream and cry every time we had to leave him.

I don't know if he was trying to fight his addictions or if he was happy with his life the way it was. Perhaps drugs and alcohol were all that really mattered to him. It certainly sometimes seemed that way, and that when he'd had to choose between his addictions and his wife and children, we had been the ones he had abandoned. He even gave up seeing my sister and me at weekends in the end, when he became so weird and unpredictable that Mum had to stop us going there.

I missed Dad a lot for a while, and then a couple of friends of Mum's and John's started coming over at the weekends with their two children and I began not to mind so much about not going to visit him. Every Saturday evening, Mum would make a huge bowl of popcorn for us kids to eat while we watched a film. Then we would go up to bed and the adults would turn on the music. I loved those weekends.

I did still miss my dad, but staying with him had started to get a bit frightening and, to be honest, I wasn't sorry not to be going there anymore. There was never anything to eat in his house and when we told him we were hungry, he just got angry and shouted at us, which made me anxious – for myself, for my little sister and for him. So it was nice to spend the weekends just being a kid at home, playing and joking around and not having to worry about anything. Until the fights started.

As I was the oldest, it felt like my responsibility to look after my sister and the two other kids who stayed with us at the weekends. So when the screaming and shouting began to kick off downstairs, and the three of them looked at me with big, scared eyes, I told them stories and pretended I wasn't frightened. The next morning, we would creep downstairs and start clearing up the mess the adults had made in the living room, in the hope that if they were pleased with us when they woke up, they wouldn't be sullen and uncommunicative with each other.

Later, when I was in Greece, I often had the same feeling of almost desperately determined optimism that I used to have on those Sunday mornings at home as we picked up the overflowing, often overturned, ashtrays, empty beer cans and bottles, and disposed of the shattered remains of whatever objects the grown-ups had hurled across the room at each other. I can still remember the feeling of heart-stopping dread I had the morning we came downstairs and found blood smeared across the living-room walls. There were words written in it, as if someone had traced the letters with their finger. I can't remember what the words were now. I just remember the way my stomach contracted painfully as I read them and that I thought I was going to be sick.

Despite the way it sounds, Mum was good at looking after us, most of the time. I know she really did want the best for my sister and me, and she worked hard to make sure we had everything we needed. I just wish she had realised at the time that all the fighting had a damaging effect – first the fights between her and Dad, and then the alcohol-fuelled rows that took place on Saturday nights with John and the couple who used to stay at our house at the weekends. Anyone who's ever woken up as a child to the sound of their parents shouting at each other will know

13

how it feels to lie awake in the darkness, listening but trying not to hear.

Sometimes, when Mum and John had had a particularly bad row, John would storm out of the house, slamming the front door behind him. He would often stay away for a few days, and while he was gone, Mum would just sit in the living room when she got home from work, watching television or listening to music and crying. It's a horrible feeling as a child to be worried about your mum or dad: you feel as if you have to do something to put things right for them, but you don't have the slightest clue what to do or how you would set about doing it even if you did.

There were many times when I wanted to hug Mum and make everything better for her. And other times when I was angry with her because she did something that made me feel anxious and frightened, although, at the time, I couldn't have put that feeling into words.

When we moved out of that house, Mum didn't want to go. But things between her and John were starting to unravel, and I think she hoped that by going along with what he wanted to do, she might be able to ward off their inevitable break-up. It didn't work, of course. We hadn't been in the new house very long when things started going from bad to worse. Mum and John were arguing almost constantly and then John lost his job and started staying at home all day, drinking. Every so often, they would have a huge row, John would storm out of the house and go to stay at his sister's, and Mum would cry and mope and play loud music. After a while, they would get back together, I would let out the breath I had been holding, and for a few days everything would be all right. Then the whole miserable cycle would start all over again.

There were fields behind the house we had moved out of; it was in a nice part of town, on a nice street where two of my best friends also lived. So I was upset when Mum told me we were moving. And I was devastated when I discovered that our new house was on a rough housing estate where, for reasons I didn't ever understand, kids like me who wouldn't say boo to a goose were picked on and sometimes physically assaulted.

The only good thing about living in that house was Dean. Dean lived next door with his parents. When my sister and I saw him for the first time on the day we moved in, he was sitting on the garden wall holding a hedgehog. We had been watching him from our new bedroom window, and then he turned round and we ducked down out of sight. But we weren't quick enough because he had already seen us, and when we looked out again he waved and beckoned for us to go outside.

Dean was a really lovely lad. I got to know him well over the next couple of years and we became good friends. It still breaks my heart when I think about how badly he was bullied and tormented by some of the other kids on that estate. He was about four years older than me, very good-looking and had a girlfriend when I first met him. Perhaps the people who made his life such a misery by repeatedly attacking his house, beating him up and spreading malicious, totally unfounded rumours about him knew before he did that he was gay.

I had always enjoyed and done well at school, so I was looking forward to moving up to secondary school. Because we had moved, I didn't go to the one I was originally meant to go to; I went to one that was local to our new house, where it didn't take the other kids long to identify me as a geek and where I was bullied almost from day one. I was put into the top set, and while my teachers praised and tried to encourage me, the kids in the playground pushed me, pulled my hair and occasionally punched me. Apparently, they didn't like the way I talked or looked or the clothes I wore – or, of course, the fact that I was a geek.

One of the reasons I had been put into the top set was because I was a quick learner. So it didn't take me long to realise that, as the bullies clearly weren't going to change their behaviour, if I wanted to fit in, I was going to have to change mine. Within just a few months of starting at the school, I was dressing differently, I had dropped my 'posh accent' and adopted all the slang words the other kids used, and I had begun to mess around in lessons.

That was the first time I put into practice my ability to hide who I really am and pretend to be someone I'm not. I hated myself for doing it, but it worked: I was put down into a lower set at school and the bullies turned their spiteful attention to other targets. What I really hated though was the fact that my teachers were disappointed with me, although not as disappointed as I was with myself, despite my apparent indifference to their concern as they asked me, repeatedly, if there was something wrong.

Now that I was on the side of the bullies, if only peripherally, I began to make friends, one of whom was a girl called Carly. Like me, Carly had started out in the top set and been moved down when her behaviour deteriorated. She was better at 'not caring' than I was though, and one day, when we had skived off school together, she took me to the car park of an office block near where she lived, pointed to a van and said, 'Let's see what's inside.' The thought of breaking into *anything* made me feel sick with anxiety. But I sensed that it was a test and if I failed it, it wouldn't be long before I was right back where I had started.

It was a stupid thing to do, particularly in a public place in broad daylight. Someone saw us and called the police, who caught us in the act and took us back to school in a police car, and then I was driven home. I was lucky to get off with a warning from the police, but I got into a whole load of trouble from my mum. Anyone who had heard me shouting back at her would never have guessed that I was embarrassed and ashamed of what I had done.

The second time the police became involved was when I was caught shoplifting make-up in a shopping mall with another friend. This time, they phoned Mum from the police station and told her to come and take me home. She was really upset and angry when she got there, and although I would have died rather than show it, I felt bad.

The police told Mum to make sure I was in court on time the next morning, and when I said that I wasn't going to go to court, one of the policemen said, 'It isn't a matter of choice. You have to go.'

'Oh yeah?' The arrogant hostility in my voice sounded convincing. 'And who's going to make me?'

The answer was that *they* were, by keeping me in a cell overnight and taking me to court the next morning in a police van. I think they had to get Mum's permission, which I'm sure she gave them willingly, in the hope that being locked in a police cell for the night might shock me into realising how it was all going to end if I didn't sort myself out pretty quickly.

By the time they dragged me, literally kicking and screaming, into the cell I really was angry. But I was scared too.

After I had done something I shouldn't have done at school one day, Mum and John were asked to come in for a meeting to discuss my behaviour. The head-teacher asked me questions about what life was like at home – as if I was going to say anything with my mum and stepdad sitting there. I don't think Mum ever understood why I was becoming increasingly unmanageable. I didn't understand it either, although I realise now that it was at least partly because there wasn't much stability in our lives at home, and because we felt as though no one really cared what we were doing or what happened to us as long as we didn't cause any trouble.

I had started running away from home. On all those occasions when Mum didn't know where I was, I think she would have been shocked if she had seen the sort of people I had become involved with. When I wasn't wandering around the estate, I was in houses where people were taking drugs, smoking weed and drinking. In fact, I didn't drink, not only because I hated the taste of alcohol, but also because of what I had seen it do to other people. I didn't take drugs either. But I did smoke, and I drove around in cars with boys being generally disruptive. I didn't do anything else with the boys except sit in their cars: under my tough façade, I was still timid and insecure and never even contemplated having any sort of emotional or sexual relationship.

Sometimes, Mum would call the police and they would come out looking for us. But they rarely found us. I didn't like Mum at that time. In fact, I didn't like anyone in my family except my sister – which anyone who heard our constant arguments might have been surprised to know. One day, when my auntie was at the house and she and Mum started laying into me about something, I just lost it. I picked up a bottle of ketchup and hurled it across the room. As it hit the wall, the bottle seemed to explode, sending shards of broken glass and disgusting red goop spraying out in all directions.

I don't know whether it was my auntie or my mum who called the police. Whoever it was, I got hauled off to the police station and kept there for a couple of hours, which made me feel obliged to keep up my act of being angry long after I didn't feel it anymore. In fact, it was horrible; it was like watching someone I didn't recognise saying vicious, nasty things. The trouble was that it had gathered its own momentum and I didn't know how to back down.

Some of my behaviour was pretty much what you would expect from a teenager going through an angry phase and starting to test the boundaries of authority. But it took on another dimension altogether when I began to self-harm, although, in fact, I only did it a couple of times. I cut myself with a razor. I don't know why. Maybe it was attention-seeking; maybe *all* my bad behaviour was really just another way of saying, 'Look at me! Do something to stop me. Don't let me get away with this.'

If I got tired of silently criticising myself, I could always turn my attention to the things I thought were wrong with Mum. I would visit friends' houses where there were framed family photographs above the fireplace and a nice car in the driveway, and I would ask Mum, 'Why can't you be like so-and-so's mum?' I think what I really wanted more than anything else was to fit in. Conforming was a big pressure, particularly on the housing estate where we lived, and I was sick of always feeling like the odd one out. I suppose that's why people hounded and tormented Dean, the boy who lived next door: they thought he was different, so they chose to ignore the fact that he was gentle, funny and clever.

Mum used to be one of those 'conforming mums', in the early days after John first came to live with us. She had a good job and was studying part-time for an NVQ. And when she wasn't working, at the weekends, she used to take my sister and me out, sometimes for lunch and then to the zoo or the cinema, and we would have really good fun. She wasn't the sort of mum who offered you her shoulder to cry on. If I ever tried to talk to her about something that was worrying or upsetting me, she would get angry and impatient. Thinking about it now, I suppose it was because she didn't know what to do about her own problems, so feeling that she had to try to solve other people's would have seemed overwhelming.

She was a terrific mum, when she was sober. It was the drink that sent everything wrong. And the drink was always there, in the background. Drinking was just what Mum and John did when they were socialising with family and friends, which was okay, until I was about 12 and it started to affect all our lives. Mum says it was John's fault, and I certainly don't think he made things better for her in the end. But I know now, from my own experiences, that you have to take responsibility for what you do and, to some extent, for what happens to you. You can't just lay all the bad stuff at someone else's door and absolve yourself of any blame.

Eventually, when I continued to miss lessons and run away from home, Mum contacted social services and asked for help. I think she hoped it would shock me into realising that life at home wasn't so bad after all. It was my anger she found particularly difficult to deal with, which I can understand, as I don't know myself why I was so angry or why I began to establish a pattern of making bad decisions.

Social services allocated a social worker, who I really liked, to me. He would talk to me and do the sort of fun things Mum and John used to do with us. So, for me, it was quite a good outcome, although the arrangement only lasted until I ran away again. This time, I went to my dad's.

I was almost 14 and it had been a few years since my sister and I had stopped spending the weekends with Dad. But when I phoned him one day, after having a row with my mum and storming out of the house, he came into town to meet me. Although I was a bit embarrassed by the fact that he was drinking beer from a can as we walked along the road together, I didn't think there was actually anything wrong with him. The truth was, however, that he had changed beyond all recognition.

He took me back to his house, where there was no electricity, no money to put in the meter, and nothing in the fridge or cupboards to eat or drink except beer. If Mum had known what things were like at Dad's, she might have sent me there herself to get the wake-up call she thought I needed. Dad wasn't bothered about the state of his house though; he didn't even seem to notice. After dropping me off, he went out again to collect my half-sister, Vicky, who was coming for an overnight visit.

When Dad came with Vicky, he asked her, 'Do you know who this is?' The last time I had seen her was almost eight years earlier, when she was a baby, not long before her mum had walked out on Dad. So she had no idea who I was. After looking at me warily for a moment, she asked, 'Is it your new girlfriend?' Dad laughed and said, 'No, stupid. It's your sister, Megan.' And Vicky burst into tears. Then she hugged me so tightly she nearly squeezed all the air out of me.

I stayed at Dad's for almost a whole, miserable month. The only thing about it that wasn't entirely negative was that it made me realise that my childhood would probably have been worse rather than better if he had stayed with us, as I had previously always wished he had done. The house was always full of his friends, just sitting around. I tried to hide the fact that most of them made me feel really uncomfortable, but he could obviously tell and he would say embarrassing things to me in front of them and then roar with laughter.

I could have gone home, but I stayed because I was still angry with Mum. She hadn't abandoned me: she wrote to me and sent Dad the child benefit she got for me every week. I know she would have been appalled if she had seen the way I was living and had known that I had stopped going to school. I don't think Dad ever even thought about how old I was and what I should actually be doing every day. And as I had obviously dropped off the radar as far as social services were concerned, I just hung around his house, like his friends did, smoking cigarettes.

I had been staying at Dad's for almost three weeks when my sister moved in too. It was really good to have her there.

Sometimes, one of the men would turn up with a child, who would be left for my sister and me to look after. We were in the bedroom one evening playing with a little boy whose father was downstairs, when a fight kicked off. We sat there for a few minutes, listening to the shouting and hoping it would stop, and then I crept down the stairs. Dad was lying on the floor of the living room in a pool of blood and one of his friends was bending over him, holding a knife and screaming, 'I'm going to kill you.' At first, I thought the man had already stabbed him and he was dead. But then he groaned and moved. I found out later that the man had taken exception to something Dad had said and picked up the TV and smashed it over his head.

I was still standing on the bottom stair, too shocked to be able to make any real sense of what had happened, when I heard a sound behind me. Spinning round, I saw my sister and the little boy huddled together and shivering. I held my finger to my lips and whispered, 'Shhh.' Then I pushed them ahead of me back up the stairs and into the bedroom. When I had closed the door silently behind me, I told them, 'We need to get out of the house. We're going

24

to have to go downstairs again.' The little boy whimpered and shook his head. 'It's all right,' I said, trying to convey a sense of confidence I didn't feel. 'Just follow me and don't make a sound.'

Everyone was still fighting and shouting as we tiptoed swiftly and silently down the stairs, across the hallway and into the kitchen. As soon as all three of us were out of the back door, we started running. We didn't stop until we reached an alleyway, where we huddled together, trying to catch our breath. Running away had been an instinctive reaction. But when I tried to think what to do next, I drew a blank. So we were still standing in the alleyway, glancing nervously over our shoulders every few seconds because we were afraid that the man with the knife might come after us, when we heard the wail of a siren. The police car was followed almost immediately by an ambulance, and by the time we crept back to the house, Dad was already being lifted on to a stretcher.

The little boy's father took him home and my sister and I were looked after for the night by neighbours. When Dad got out of hospital, my sister went back to live with him again. But I had already decided that I was going to go home to Mum.

It was a good decision, in theory. In practice, it would prove to be a case of out of the frying pan, into the fire.

Chapter 2

Mum and John had split up while I was staying at Dad's, for good this time. Despite mostly blaming John for what had happened, I know Mum was really upset and that she missed him. I was sorry too: I always wished things could have gone back to the way they used to be in the early days of their relationship.

I think Mum was depressed and lonely before I came home, so she was glad to have me back. We got on a lot better than we had done before I went away and became really close – partly, I suppose, because I had grown up a bit in the month I had been living at Dad's.

Shortly after I returned home, my sister was taken into care. I had just turned 14 and should have been in school, so they were probably looking for me too. Despite having made friends, both on the housing estate and at school, before I had gone to live with Dad, I hadn't completely escaped from the bullying. So I had no reason to want things to go back to the way they had been. It seemed as though life had stalled for Mum and for me. And then Mum announced that we were going on holiday to Greece.

I've often wondered what would have happened if Dad hadn't started drinking, if we had stayed together as a family living in the nice house we used to live in, and if my sister and I had finished school and maybe gone to university. I know that was what Mum wanted for us – a good education that would lead to us getting good jobs. Our lives might even have been different if John and Mum had worked things out and stayed together.

I do have some happy memories of the early days after John moved in. For example, we used to have a party at our house every New Year's Eve. Everyone would be cheerful and laughing, and even when they all got a bit drunk, no one was ever angry or shouted. Then we moved to the new house, everything changed and I began to wish we could turn back the clock so that Mum could make some different decisions. But we couldn't, so there was no point being miserable about how things might have been.

I hated leaving my sister behind in England when Mum and I went to Greece. I would have been glad that she wasn't coming with us if I had known what was going to happen when we got there. I had never been abroad before.

I was so excited I could hardly sit still on the plane. When we arrived at the airport in Greece, we got a taxi to the small, basic but clean apartment Mum had rented. As soon as we had dumped our bags and done a little dance around the room, we went to the beach. The sand was golden, the water was warm and crystal clear; in fact, everything about the place we were staying was just the way I had imagined it would be, but better.

That first evening, we went to a bar right next to the beach, and as Mum and I sat laughing and talking, I felt more relaxed than I had done for a long time. I still didn't drink alcohol, but that night I had a couple of Bacardi Breezers – and then went back to coke when Mum realised I was getting a bit tipsy. We danced and chatted to other tourists and to the bar owner, who spoke really good English and entertained everyone by mixing cocktails and telling jokes.

There were three guys sitting at a table near the back of the room and whenever I glanced surreptitiously in their direction, one of them seemed to be watching me. He was the best dressed and the best looking of the three, and when he caught my eye I got a fluttery feeling in my stomach. It was one of the other two who came over and asked Mum and me to dance. In fact, he didn't really *ask* us; he was Albanian and didn't speak any English, so he just kept repeating the word 'Hello' and then did a sort of mime that made us laugh. We did dance with him – by that time everyone in the bar was dancing and chatting with everyone else – and he seemed like a nice guy. But I was more interested in his friend.

It was late by the time Mum and I went back to the apartment. I fell asleep thinking about the guy I hadn't spoken to, and maybe Mum dreamed about the bar owner, who had clearly been attracted to her and whose attention had made her giggle like a schoolgirl.

The next day, we went to the beach again, ate our lunch sitting in the sun outside a café, and then returned in the evening to the same bar, where the same three guys were sitting at the table they had been sitting at the night before. As soon as we sat down, Zef, the guy who had danced with us the previous evening, came over and asked me – again by the use of mime – if I wanted a drink. And after he had bought me a coke, he introduced me to his two friends.

All three of the men were in their early to mid-twenties. One of Zef's two friends was called Veli; the other shook my hand and then held it for a few seconds while he looked directly into my eyes and told me, in broken English, that his name was Jak. Although I didn't think for a moment that someone like Jak would ever fancy someone like me, I felt my knees go weak.

Mum had also had a reason for wanting to go back to the bar that night, and while I was sitting with Zef, Veli and Jak, she was talking to the Greek bar owner, Nikos. In fact, she was having such a good time I think she barely noticed when we left the bar at around 2 o'clock in the morning to go down to the beach. I knew Zef wanted me to go on the back of *his* motorcycle, but although he was obviously a nice guy, his faltering eagerness didn't appeal to me the way his friend's self-confidence did. So I went with Jak.

For the next couple of hours, we sat on the still-warm sand smoking cigarettes and talking. Then they dropped me back at the bar and Mum and I walked together up the road to the apartment. The chaotic life I had been living in England suddenly seemed a very long way away.

The days and nights developed a pattern after that. In the morning and afternoon, Mum and I would swim and lie on the beach. Then we would go back to the apartment to shower and get changed before having our dinner in a café or at one of the restaurants that lined the square in the centre of town. And then we would go to Nikos's bar. I loved spending time with my mum, lying on the beach, laughing, talking and relaxing as the warmth of the sun eased all the tension out of my muscles.

Mum had made quite a few friends at the bar among both local people and tourists. So she was happy to leave me to do whatever I wanted in the evenings, which was mostly to sit on the beach with Jak and his friends. She did have one concern though. 'I don't like Jak's eyes,' she told me. 'There's something dead and cold about them. I don't think I've ever seen him smile, have you?'

'Oh, Mum,' I replied, groaning and raising my eyebrows.

'Well, I'm just saying,' she said. 'There's definitely something dodgy about him – whereas Zef seems like a really sweet boy, and he's obviously keen on you. I'd stay away from Jak if I were you, and think about Zef instead.'

I wonder if any parent has ever managed to persuade their son or daughter to 'stay away' from someone they're attracted to and to transfer their affections to someone the parent thinks is more suitable. Somehow I doubt it! And I wonder how many of those sons and daughters look back later on a specific piece of advice their parents gave them and think, 'If only I'd listened.' But you don't listen to anyone when you're young – expect perhaps to your friends, whose ideas are likely to be as half-cooked as your own – because you think you know it all. For me, in this particular instance, it was too late anyway: I was already smitten with Jak and I completely ignored what was probably the best piece of advice my mum has ever given me.

By mid-week, Jak had started coming to find us on the beach during the day. He only spoke half a dozen words of English, so we communicated – surprisingly well – using a sort of sign language. What he did say quite clearly one day though was, 'Baby, I love you,' and when he kissed me I thought I was going to pass out. We were together almost constantly. He had already told me several times that he didn't want me to leave, and when he cried on our last evening, it almost broke my heart. The thought that he even 'approved' of me, let alone might be attracted to me, made me believe that there might just be a possibility that my life wasn't to going to end up being the disaster I had begun to think it might be.

At the airport the next day, both Mum and I were very quiet. Things had been going really well between her and Nikos too, and I knew she was as miserable as I was. We had checked in for our flight and were walking across the concourse towards the entrance to the departure area when I stopped, put my hand on her arm and said, 'Please Mum, can't we stay? I don't want to go home. What have I got to go back for? Please, just think about it.' I began to cry, but Mum just sighed and said, 'I know, Megan. I feel the same way. But we don't have any choice. Come on, love. We've got to go.'

'But, Mum …' Not many days earlier, I would probably have thrown a full-scale tantrum and have had to be dragged to the plane kicking and screaming. This time though, the thing I wanted – which was not to have to leave Jak – *really* mattered to me and I knew instinctively that a fit of teenage temper wasn't the way to get it.

'But, Mum …' I sniffed pathetically and looked at her with what I hoped was a sad and at the same time sympathetic expression. 'How can you even think of leaving Nikos when he loves you?'

'What do you mean?' She sounded almost embarrassed, and there was a wistful look in her eyes as she added, 'Nikos doesn't love me.'

'Yes he does!' I said, feeling like a fisherman must feel when there's a small but definite tug on his line. 'He told me so last night. He said he didn't want you to go, but he didn't know what to do to stop you.'

'Did he?' When I saw the tears in Mum's eyes, I don't think I could have felt any worse if I had actually hit her.

'Yeah, he was really upset.' I couldn't look at her as I said the words.

How could I have lied like that to my mum? It's a question I've asked myself a million times and it still makes me cry when I think about it today. It was selfish and, as it turned out, incredibly stupid from my own point of view. Because if I hadn't said what I said to her as we stood in the airport in Greece that day, we would have gone home, my broken heart would have mended itself in time, and although the rest of my life might not have been particularly happy or exciting, I wouldn't have had to endure the six years of hell I had just opened the door to.

I could tell that Mum had made a decision – she had that look on her face children have when they're going to do something naughty. And when she said, 'Come on then,' and started striding purposefully back towards the check-in desk, I scuttled along behind her with my heart racing.

'I'm sorry,' she told the woman at the desk. 'But we've decided not to go on this flight after all.'

'*I'm* sorry,' the woman said, 'but it's too late. Your bags have already gone through.' She flashed a frosty smile at Mum that said quite clearly, 'I'm exerting a huge amount of self-control to prevent myself addressing you as "Stupid".'

'Please.' Mum appeared oblivious to the woman's disdain. 'Isn't there anything you can do? My daughter and I *need* to stay here, just for another week. Please.'

I don't know what it was that made the woman change her mind. Perhaps she wasn't really as tough and indifferent as she seemed and she felt sorry for us, huddled there, tearful and pathetic, at her check-in desk. Whatever the reason, she did manage to stop our two large suitcases being loaded on to the plane, and a few minutes later we were standing in the heat outside the airport wondering what to do next.

Mum had spent all the money in her bank account in England, and wouldn't have any more until her last wages were paid into it. So we couldn't even afford to get a taxi. In the end, we walked a short distance down the road, hid our suitcases in some bushes – having agreed to work out later how we were going to get them back – and then tried to hitch a lift. It wasn't much of a plan, but we couldn't think of a better one. And we were lucky, because someone did stop to pick us up and even agreed to take us back to the town on the coast where we had been staying.

The man dropped us outside a restaurant we had eaten in a few times, which was on the same road as Nikos's bar. When we got out of his car, Mum straightened her skirt, took a deep breath and said, 'I feel so nervous. What am I going to say to him?' I had hardly said anything all the time we had been in the car because I felt so bad about what I had done. Now, I started to cry. 'I'm sorry,' I told Mum. 'I lied. Nikos didn't actually say he loved you.' She just stood there for a moment, completely still, as if her whole body had frozen. 'But I really think he does,' I added hastily. 'I could see how upset he was whenever you talked about leaving.'

When she did finally look at me, she had an expression on her face as if she didn't recognise me. She burst into tears and sat down heavily on a chair outside the restaurant, and still didn't say anything until she had ordered a drink and swallowed a large mouthful of it. Then she said, 'Oh Megan, what have you done?'

'I'm so sorry, Mum. I just panicked at the thought of going back to England. Everything's been so different – for both of us – since we came here. I've had the best time I've had for years. And I know you have too. I *know* Nikos really likes you, and he's such a nice guy. So why go home to nothing when you've got someone like him here? I'm sure it'll be okay.' I sounded certain, but in reality the doubts had already crept in and I wasn't at all sure that things would turn out well for either of us. Fortunately, Mum was too shocked to be angry with me, and after we had finished our drinks, we walked together down the road to Nikos's bar.

Mum stopped outside the bar and stood for a few seconds, just breathing. Then she made a sort of gulping-sob sound and walked through the beaded curtain that hung in the open doorway. Nikos was setting up the bar ready for the customers who would come that evening. When he heard the rattle of the curtain, he turned towards the door with a bland smile and I think my heart stopped beating. Then suddenly, as he realised it was us, he threw down the cloth he was holding and almost ran towards us, enveloping first my mother and then me in a huge hug.

'We decided to stay another week,' Mum said nervously when she could breathe again.

'I'm so happy,' Nikos kept saying. 'I'm working in my bar wishing you hadn't had to leave and now here you are! Where are you staying?'

'We haven't got anywhere yet, but ...' Mum sounded embarrassed.

'It's no problem,' Nikos interrupted her. 'I will sort it out.'

He poured a drink for Mum, flipped the top off a bottle of coke for me and then made a phone call. Within minutes, everything was arranged. Mum and I would be staying in an apartment that was owned by one of his friends – and which turned out to be large and spacious with a sea view. When Mum told him what we had done with our suitcases, Nikos laughed and then he drove us back to the airport to retrieve them from the bushes. For the next few days, until Mum's wages were in her bank account in England, he also fed us and paid the rent on our apartment.

Having seen Nikos's reaction to Mum's return, I was very nervous, as well as excited, at the prospect of seeing Jak again. I didn't have to wait long: he came into the bar that evening and was as surprised and happy to see me as I could have hoped.

Over the next few days, Mum's relationship with Nikos and mine with Jak developed so well that she didn't book a flight back to England for us the following week, as she had intended. In fact, it was another six weeks before she made any plans for us to go home.

A couple of days after we had hitch-hiked back from the airport, Jak picked me up from the apartment and took me to meet his family, who lived in a small house in the countryside. None of them spoke any English, but as his mother fussed around me, clicking her tongue and poking me with her bony fingers, I learned the Albanian words for 'too thin'. What I hadn't understood, however, was that she intended to set about the task of fattening me up immediately.

It had already been agreed that Jak and I would stay for lunch, and we had just sat down at the table when his mother came out of the kitchen carrying a large plate. She stood beside me and held it up close to my face, and as I turned my head to look at it, she pushed her fingers into the mouth of the boiled goat's head and pulled out its tongue, nodding her own head as she did so and making an appreciative sort of humming noise. I think being in such close proximity to the head of a dead goat would have been repulsive even if I hadn't been brought up as a vegetarian. Fortunately, I just managed to turn my head away from the plate as I was violently sick.

The embarrassment I already felt at being the object of everyone's close scrutiny was nothing compared with my mortification at having emptied the contents of my stomach all over the floor. I had desperately wanted Jak's family to like me. But by the time I had finished vomiting and retching, his sister didn't even try to hide her irritation as she clicked her tongue impatiently and pushed me towards the bathroom.

'I'm sorry,' I kept saying. 'I'm so sorry.' But his mother had already fetched a mop and bucket from the kitchen to clear up the mess I had made and I don't know if she even heard me.

After lunch – none of which I was able to eat – they seemed to get over the worst of their annoyance and we sat outside the house, drinking juice and listening to Albanian music. They spoke to me in Albanian, and as Jak could only translate the odd word into English, we communicated mostly using mime and drawings. I'm shy and quite easily intimidated, whereas they were noisily dramatic. So I was relieved when Jak said it was time to go, and took me back to the apartment on his motorbike.

A few days after I had visited Jak's family, Mum talked to me about sex. I can't remember exactly what she said, except that she wanted me to wait. 'Just leave it for now, Megan,' she told me. 'But when you *do* do it, make sure you use a condom.' I can understand why it was a discussion she thought we needed to have, but I wasn't planning to 'do it' at all. I could be stubborn and stroppy as a teenager, but I was very naïve. I was a virgin when I went with Mum to Greece, and the idea of having sex with *anyone* had never even crossed my mind. It was love not sex that I was so desperate for, although of course I didn't realise that at the time.

In fact, I had been put off the whole idea of sex when I was 12. I had visited someone's house and they had shown me a porn video. I had only watched a few minutes of it; it was violent and completely alien to anything I had imagined was involved in falling in love, and I found it very disturbing. After that, sex became inextricably linked in my mind to things that were traumatic and disgusting. So by the time I went to stay at my dad's and he started saying vulgar, horrible things to me and trying to get me to sleep with his friends, I had made an almost subconscious decision to avoid having sex for as long as I possibly could.

It was during the third week of our extended stay that Dean, my friend and our next-door neighbour in England, came out to stay at the apartment with Mum and me for a few days. I was really excited when he said he was coming and to begin with I loved having him there. Late at night, after the bars had closed, we would all go down to the beach together – me, Dean, Jak and his friends – and talk until the sun came up.

Dean got on really well with Zef and after a couple of days he asked me, as Mum had done, 'Why do you like Jak more than Zef? I don't understand your attraction to him at all. He never smiles and he's got this really hard look in his eyes. I don't like him, and I certainly wouldn't trust him.' I don't think I would have listened to anyone by that point, because I was already hooked. What was really sad, though, was that what Dean said that day affected our previously easy, relaxed relationship, and we didn't get on so well for the rest of the week he was there. I lost touch with him after he returned to England, which is something I now deeply regret, because it meant that I didn't see him again before he killed himself a couple of years ago.

What human traffickers do is evil and despicable, but I suppose it makes cold, hard, financial sense to the criminals involved to trade the lives of people they don't know or care about in exchange for monetary gain. What I really don't understand is what the pay-off is for bullies. It seems that, for people like the ones who persecuted and tormented Dean and ultimately destroyed his life, the goal is, purely and simply, to cause distress. In some ways, that almost makes them worse than human traffickers and drug dealers, for whom ruining other people's lives is simply a by-product of businesses that earn them vast sums of money.

When Jak came to pick me up from the apartment one day, not long after Dean had returned to England, he handed me a carrier bag and said solemnly, 'For you.' Inside the bag there was a blue vest top and a pair of cut-off cotton trousers.

'They're very nice,' I said. 'But why are you giving me clothes?'

'You need them,' he answered, and then shrugged. 'My mother, she buys them for you. *She* says you need them.'

'Your English is getting good,' I laughed. But I was embarrassed, because I knew his family was poor.

Jak took me to a café, where he pointed to the toilet and told me to go and try on my new outfit. I was surprised to find that the clothes fitted me really well, and I was pleased by his reaction when I walked back into the café wearing them. After we'd had a cup of coffee, he took me on his motorbike to his house, where his mother made me turn around while she adjusted the top to make it sit perfectly on my shoulders. Then she said something that Jak translated for me as, 'You look just like Albanian girl.' I blushed, because I was embarrassed by his mother's attention and because it felt as though, despite the goat's head incident, she had decided after all to accept me into her family, and that seemed like something very special and comforting.

I think it was on that day that I considered for perhaps the first time the possibility that my life might actually turn out to be different from what I had begun to believe it would be. I hardly dared believe it when Jak kissed me and told me he loved me as he dropped me back at the apartment every night. I was grateful to him for being patient and gentle with me, and for the fact that he never pressured me to have sex. I had already fallen head over heels for him, and on the day when his mother bought me clothes and seemed to be giving me her seal of approval, I looked at him and thought, 'This is the man I want to be with. This is what I want for the rest of my life.'

So it was an easy decision to make when, a few days later, he asked me to leave the apartment I had been sharing with Mum and move in with him and his family for the rest of our stay in Greece.

Chapter 3

Although Mum still didn't like or trust Jak, she didn't have any real objections to my going to live with him and his family – I suppose because she knew his parents would be there. She was spending most of her time with Nikos, but I continued to see or talk to her almost every day after I moved out of the apartment.

Jak was working as a gardener and I was able to go with him, to sit in the sun and talk to him while he did his jobs. It was about two weeks after Mum and I had not taken our flight home that I began to notice how much better his English was. 'I learn really quick,' he told me when I remarked on his rapid improvement. And I had no reason to doubt what he said.

He often told me: 'I don't want you ever to go home. I want you to stay here with me for ever. I love you.' And

I believed that too. I really wanted it to be true, because I knew that I loved him. At the age of 14, I think the only ambition I had ever had was to know that someone had chosen to love me.

I only stayed with Jak's family for a few days before Jak and I moved into a small apartment in a town a bit further along the coast. I didn't tell Mum though. I let her go on believing that we were still living with his parents. Jak and I had been in the new place for just a couple of days when we had a huge row. I had told him I wasn't going to go to work with him that morning because I wanted to spend some time with my mum, and he looked really hurt and asked, 'Why don't you want to spend the day with me?'

'I've spent every day with you,' I said, 'and I'll see you this evening. But today I want to see my mum.'

I was completely taken by surprise when he suddenly started shouting at me. I didn't understand everything he was saying, because the angrier he got the more he seemed to lose his grasp of English. And then he bellowed into my face, 'You don't love me! I want to spend *all* the time with you, but you don't want that.'

I might have been pleased to think he felt jealous if I had been planning to spend the day with someone else. But it was my mother I wanted to see, and his aggressive reaction startled me. I hadn't entirely lost the stroppy teenager part of my character so I shouted back at him. And when our neighbours complained to the landlord about the loud, full-scale argument that ensued, we were kicked out of the apartment the next day.

Jak was contrite about his jealousy, and I was flattered when he told me that the reason he was so upset was because he loved me so much he wanted me to be with him all the time. What I didn't realise, of course, was that far from simply being a stupid row, it was actually the start of his determined efforts to separate me from my mother.

Not long after we had moved into another apartment – a few streets away in the same town – Mum told me she had booked seats for us on another flight back to England. Apparently, she hadn't paid rent on our council house for the last six weeks and a friend of hers had phoned to say that the people from the council had been in, cleared everything out of it, dumped all our stuff in a skip and changed the locks.

'I don't want to leave,' I told Mum. 'There really *is* nothing for us to go back for now.'

But she was adamant. 'I don't want to go either,' she said. 'But we've got to. It'll only be for a few weeks. Once we've sorted things out at home, we'll come back again.'

Everything was going really well between Mum and Nikos, so I knew she had as many reasons to want to stay as I did. Even a few weeks seemed like a very long time to me though, particularly when I already knew from experience how quickly and irrevocably things can change.

Jak was really upset when I told him. 'I don't know how I'll survive if you leave me,' he said, in his now-excellent English.

The night before our flight, Jak drank quite a lot of whisky and cried as he told me, 'I will suffer so much if I have to live without you even for a few weeks.' Then, with tears streaming down his face, he stubbed out his cigarette on his arm. I was frightened by the passion of his distress, but I was thrilled by it too and by the thought that he really did love me and that he felt as miserable as I did at the prospect of us being apart.

Despite sleeping in the same bed during the weeks we had been together, Jak and I still hadn't had sex, although we had come close to it a few times. That was something else I really liked about him – the fact that as soon as he sensed I was getting tense, he always backed off. I slept badly that night, and every time I woke up and felt his arms around me, I dreaded the prospect of being alone again.

The next morning, Mum and Nikos took my suitcase to the airport in Nikos's car, and I went with Jak on the back of his motorbike. When he pulled up outside the terminal, I swung my leg over the seat and as I turned to give him a last kiss, I saw that he was crying.

'Don't go, Megan,' he said, holding my face in his hands and looking deep into my own tear-filled eyes. 'I love you so much. Please don't go. Get back on the bike and we'll drive away from here and go and live our lives together.

Please, Megan. I love you.' And that's when I realised I couldn't leave him.

We were already speeding along the road away from the airport when Jak's phone started to ring. It kept on ringing until he stopped the bike and answered it. After listening impassively for a few seconds, he handed the phone to me, saying, 'Speak to your mum. She's very angry.'

I could hear Mum's voice even before I held the phone to my ear and I could tell that she was upset too. 'Where *are* you, Megan?' she said. 'People are starting to go the departure gate. We're going to miss our flight if you don't come *now*. What are you doing? Please, Megan.'

'I'm not coming,' I told her, unnerved by the fact that my resolve had started to crumble as soon as I heard her voice. But I knew it was already too late to change my mind. 'I'm not coming back, Mum. I can't leave Jak. I love him and he loves me. We're going to make a life together.'

'For God's sake, Megan …' Her voice was drowned out for a moment by the tinny echo of a flight announcement. When she spoke again I could tell that she was crying. 'Please, Megan, don't do this,' she pleaded. 'Come home with me now. We'll come back, I promise.'

'I love him, Mum,' I said again, wiping the tears from my cheeks with the back of my hand.

'I don't think you understand.' Mum sounded angry now. 'For God's sake, Megan, you're 14 years old. This isn't a decision you can make. If you don't come back to the airport right now and catch this flight with me, I'm going to have to go to the police.'

I didn't know how to respond, how to make her understand there was no way that I was going back.

'Megan, listen to me, you need to come home. You cannot stay here by yourself!' I could tell that she was starting to panic. 'Megan, *please*. They're calling our flight!'

'I can't come home,' I said, tears now streaming down my cheeks. 'I'll kill myself if you try to make me go home. I mean it, Mum. I want to be with Jak.' I didn't hear what she said after that, because I turned off the phone.

It still makes me cry when I think about that phone call. I don't blame my mum for leaving without me. My decision to stay in Greece took her (and me) completely by surprise, and my heartfelt threat to kill myself must have sent her into such a tailspin of panic that she didn't know what else to do.

After Jak had taken the phone out of my shaking hands, he drove to a block of apartments where a friend of his called Vasos lived. As soon as we were inside, I began to sob. Jak kept hugging me and telling me everything would be all right. But suddenly I couldn't imagine how I was going to live without my mum. I felt terrible for having upset her so much, and although just a few minutes earlier I had believed that if I had to leave Jak I would never be happy again, I now felt scared and was already regretting the decision I had made.

'I just need a minute,' I told Jak, and as I stepped out on to the balcony, I saw the plane. It seemed to be ascending very slowly into the sky above a distant row of rooftops, and as it came closer I could see the distinctive colours of the airline on its tail and I knew it was the plane I should have been on with my mother. Plummeting from distress into hysteria, I began to wave frantically and shout, 'Mum, I'm here. Can you see me? Come back. Don't leave me here. Please, Mum. I'm sorry. Don't go home without me.'

For a moment, I almost believed I could see her face looking out of one of the windows of the plane, and that she could see me standing on the balcony. Then a wave of panic washed over me and I couldn't breathe. I tugged at the handle of the balcony door, shouting, 'I want my mum,' and ran out of the apartment, down the stairs and on to the street. I kept on running until I reached the end of the road, where I sank to my knees on the hot, stony pavement, sobbing, 'I'm sorry, Mum. Please come back.'

When Jak caught up with me, I was still waving frantically at what was now an empty sky. 'Come on. Come back inside. You'll be okay,' he told me, putting his arms around my shaking body and lifting me on to my feet before half-carrying me back up the road.

When we were inside the apartment again, Jak handed me a mug of hot chocolate and said, 'Drink this. Then go and have a shower. It will make you feel better.' It didn't, though, and for the rest of day I sat staring at the wall of the living room while the two men watched television.

My suitcase had been loaded on to the plane with Mum's this time, so I had nothing except my handbag and the clothes I was wearing. 'I'll buy you something tomorrow,' Jak said when we were lying beside each other in bed that night. But even though I knew what I had done wasn't his fault, I felt sick and pulled away from him when he tried to touch me.

'I'm not ready,' I told him.

'I understand,' he said. 'I love you.'

When I woke up the next morning, no less exhausted than I had been the night before, Jak and Vasos were getting ready for work.

'You stay here,' Jak said. 'You can clean up the apartment.' I felt numb and the day passed incredibly slowly. I couldn't eat or think about anything except my mum. Where would she be now? What would she be doing? How would she be feeling?

'She's coming back,' I kept telling myself. 'I'll see her again very soon.' Even though I knew it was true, it didn't make me feel any better, and as the hours dragged by, I became increasingly anxious to talk to her. So when Jak got back from work that evening and told me he'd had a text from her and that I should call, I almost snatched the phone out of his hand.

'I've been so worried about you,' Mum said. 'Just take care of yourself. I'll be back as soon as possible, I promise.'

I felt much calmer after I had spoken to her. I knew I was really going to miss her, but it was stupid of me to have got into such a state about it all, particularly when I had Jak to look after me until she came back. And I really was all right, once I knew Mum wasn't worried to death about me and that I would be able to text and speak to her on Jak's phone every day.

For the next couple of weeks, our lives fell into an easy pattern. I would either go with Jak to work or stay at Vasos's apartment during the day. Then, in the evening, after we'd had something to eat, we would go out for a coffee. I would often tell Jak how impressed I was by the extraordinarily rapid improvement in his English, and he'd respond by teaching me some more words in Albanian and telling me how proud he was of me when I repeated them back to him.

One evening, as we were sitting outside a café in a square in the centre of town, Jak's phone rang. He listened before speaking rapidly in Albanian for a few seconds. Then he put the phone down on the table and sighed.

'What's wrong?' I asked him, touching the warm skin of his arm with my fingers. 'Has something happened? Are you all right?'

'I've just had some bad news,' he said. 'My mother is very ill.' His eyes filled with tears.

'Oh no, I'm so sorry.' I gripped his arm tightly. 'What's wrong with her?'

'It's cancer.' He spread out his hands with their palms turned upwards in a gesture of helplessness. 'It's in her throat. The doctor thought it was … How do you call it?' He touched his neck. '*Tiroide*?'

51

'Thyroid?' I said.

He nodded miserably. 'They did some tests and now they've told her today that it is cancer.'

'Oh, Jak, that's terrible! Can it be treated?'

The sound he made was like a burst of angry laughter. 'Yes, it can be treated, for someone who can afford to have an operation. This isn't England, you know. Just visiting a doctor here costs fifty euros. I can't even imagine what the operation would cost.' He rubbed his face with his hand and wiped away the tears that were falling openly now. 'My parents don't have any money. You know that. And it takes me a whole day to earn fifty euros, even though I work very hard.' He sighed again and I tried to think of something comforting to say, but couldn't. 'Well, I'm just going to have to get a second job,' he said at last. 'I just hope I can earn enough money to pay for the treatment my mother needs before … before it's too late. I don't have any choice: you can't just stand by and watch someone you love suffer and then die.'

I was crying too by that time. I had always had the sense that Jak's mother didn't really like me, but that didn't affect the fact that I felt incredibly sorry for her, and for Jak too. I knew he was very fond of his mother, and I couldn't even begin to imagine how I would feel if *my* mum was ever seriously ill. What I didn't know until a long time later was that Jak could have won an Oscar for his performance that evening.

I think he had already decided we were going to move back in with his family. So that's what we did a couple of days later. It wasn't what I wanted to do, but I certainly wasn't going to argue about it, given the circumstances. Sometimes, I would see him touch his mum's throat as he was talking to her. Otherwise, neither she nor anyone else in the family gave any indication that she was ill.

I didn't go to work with Jak anymore. I stayed in the house and helped his mum and sister do the heavy-duty housework that they taught me to do *their* way, with often unconcealed disdain for my lack of knowledge.

Jak's parents slept in the only proper bed in the house, and every day the mattress had to be lifted off it, carried outside and beaten with a sort of carpet beater made out of cane and shaped like a tennis racquet. Then the mattress was left to air before being put back on the bed again, topside down. On most days, all the sheets and bed covers were hung out to air too, except on wash days, when they had to be taken out into the garden to be scrubbed and rubbed in freezing cold water in a metal tub until your knuckles were raw and bleeding.

However hard I worked, it seemed that I could never do anything the way some unwritten law stated that it must be done. One day, after I had struggled to lift something that was way beyond the limits of my strength, Jak's mother clicked her tongue and said something to Jak, which he translated for me as, 'English girls are very dirty.' It seemed unfair, as well as irrelevant to the current task. What hurt me most of all was the fact that Jak's tone of voice suggested he might agree with what his mother said.

Ever since I was a very small child, the thing I think I wanted more than almost anything else was for people to like me. So I particularly hated being around Jak's dad, because he made no attempt at all to hide his impatient dislike of me. Whenever he walked into a room and found me there, he would glare at me, make angry clicking noises with his tongue and then say something unmistakably nasty in Albanian before walking out again. It might not have been because he was irritated with me personally, however. He wasn't much nicer to his wife, who he continued to bully even now that she was ill.

At every mealtime, everyone would sit down at the table while Jak's mum served the food and then stood up to eat hers. When it happened the first time, I jumped up and offered her my chair. She glared at me as though I had done something contemptible, and glanced anxiously at her husband, who muttered something angry, and Jak almost shouted at me, 'What do you think you're doing? She stands up.' I seemed to have done something insulting in some way I didn't understand and I felt really embarrassed. So I asked Jak later, 'Why do you let your dad treat your mum like that? I don't understand why a man would make a woman stand up to eat. That doesn't happen in England. Everyone sits at the table together.'

'It's the Albanian culture,' he snapped at me. 'In Albania, wives love their husbands and husbands love their wives. Perhaps that's something that doesn't happen in England either. In Albania women do everything for their men.

That's what we call family.' I realised I didn't have enough normal family experience to be able to argue with him. But it seemed to me to be a very strange way to treat someone you loved.

As the days passed, I became more and more miserable, until eventually I told Jak I was unhappy living with his family and asked him if we could get a place of our own. It felt like proof of his love for me when he agreed, and a couple of days later we moved out. The one-room apartment Jak rented for us was tiny, although I think by that time I would have been happy living in a shed or a tent as long as it meant not having to put up with his family's disapproval and the constant feeling that I wasn't good enough in almost every way.

It was shortly after we moved into the apartment that I began to see the first glimpses of another side of Jak. Perhaps it was the side of him my mum had thought she could see in his face and in the 'hardness' in his eyes that prompted her – and Dean – to try to persuade me not to fall for him.

Jak and I had had some loud, shouted arguments, but nothing worse than the sort of rows I used to have with my mum and sister. After we moved into the apartment, however, he would sometimes be moody when he got home from work and would get angry about apparently trivial things – for example, if his dinner wasn't on the table as soon as he walked through the door. 'That's the Albanian way,' he would tell me. So, because I loved him and because I wanted him to love and approve of me, I told myself he was right and that 'the Albanian way' was indeed the best way of doing things.

During the time we were living with his family, Jak's mum used to tell me to 'watch and learn' while she cooked, and after we moved out I tried to remember how to make the meals she made. One day, I decided to make a sort of soup-stew she used to make out of rice, spinach, boiled chicken and lemon. There was no kitchen in the apart-ment, just a sink and a small, two-ring electric hob in one corner of the room that was also our living-room/bedroom.

I was stirring the food in a pot on the hob when Jak got home from work. I could see he was tired and hungry. But nothing could have prepared me for what happened next. I had just picked up a ladle and was about to transfer the soupy stew into two bowls when he said, with a terseness that took me by surprise, 'Leave it. I'll do it myself.' Dipping a spoon into the pot, he tasted the food and then stood there for a moment, still holding the spoon to his lips. It was as if every muscle in his body had frozen and when he did finally turn his head to look at me, there was a horrible expression on his face I had never seen before and couldn't interpret. I had expected him to be pleased because I'd tried to make something his mother used to make, some-thing I knew he really liked. I couldn't think of any reason at all why he might be as angry as he clearly was. But suddenly my palms were sweating and I felt sick.

Turning very slowly away from the little stove, Jak shouted, 'You don't even know how to cook! Have you learned *nothing* from my mother?' And he picked up the pot and hurled it across the room.

It smashed against the wall just above my head, its boiling contents spewed out in every direction. As I pulled off the stew-spattered cotton top I was wearing, I screamed at him, 'What are you doing? Are you crazy?' I was so shocked that although my whole body was shaking, I didn't cry at first. Then, like a child suddenly realising she's out of her depth in some way she doesn't understand, I began to wail, 'I want to go home. I want my mum.'

It was as if a switch had been flipped inside Jak, shutting off his fury and turning on his anguished tears. 'I'm sorry,' he kept saying. 'I'm so sorry. I don't know what came over me.'

'I don't care,' I shouted at him. 'I want my mum.'

'No, please, I'm sorry.' He took a step towards me with his arms outstretched. 'I will teach you how to cook. It's all right. I'm not like that. It's just that I'm so worried about my mother. I'm upset because I can't do anything to help her.'

Fortunately, apart from a few patches on my back, I wasn't badly burned. After I had washed all the chicken, rice and spinach out of my hair and changed my clothes, Jak took me out for a meal. When we had eaten, we drove up into the mountains on his motorbike, where we sat together on a rock at the side of the road, talking and looking down on the flickering lights along the coast. Jak pointed at a cluster of stars and said, 'Those are *our* stars. Whatever happens in the future, wherever you are, you can look up at those stars and know that I am looking at them too, and that I'm thinking about you.' And by the time we drove back down the mountain in the darkness, he had soothed my anxieties and reclaimed my trust.

Chapter 4

A few evenings after my attempt to make a nice meal for Jak had ended so badly, we were sitting outside a café drinking coffee when he asked me, 'How would you feel about working? If you were earning money, we could pay for the treatment my mum needs, then buy a car and start saving for our own house. We'll need a place of our own if we're going to have children.'

I wasn't yet 15, and Jak and I still hadn't had sex, but the thought that he loved me and wanted us to have a family made me incredibly happy. Because of Jak, I was going to be able to put my own turbulent childhood behind me and, in effect, start my life again.

'I would *love* to work,' I told him. 'I don't know what I could do, but, yes, definitely.'

'Oh, there are lots of jobs you could do,' he said. 'You could do cleaning, or waitressing, or …'

'I've always thought it would be fun to be a waitress,' I interrupted him.

'Good.' He nodded approvingly. 'I'll call my cousin Mergim now and see what he can set up for you.'

While Jak was talking on the phone to his cousin, I drank my coffee and tried to picture in my mind the café or taverna where I would soon be serving food to friendly, cheerful customers who left me large tips.

'It's done,' Jak told me a few minutes later. 'Mergim can arrange a job for you in Athens.'

'Really? Oh Jak, that's so exciting! I can't wait.'

'In fact, there are a few jobs you can choose from,' he said. 'We can decide when we get there. Then we can get an apartment …'

I couldn't believe we were really going to go to Athens! It would be like stepping out of the past into a future that would be different in almost every respect. The next morning, Jak packed a suitcase with his own things and with the clothes he had bought for me after almost everything I owned had gone back to England with Mum. Then we got a taxi to the coach station, where we sat together drinking coffee and waiting to get on the bus that would take us to our new life.

The journey to Athens took several hours. Jak's cousin had said he would pick us up from the coach station. But he phoned while we were en route and said he had some business to tie up and that Jak should get a taxi to his apartment, where he would meet us.

Mergim lived in the centre of the city, in a large apartment that seemed to be full of members of his family, who all fussed over me when Jak introduced me to them. Although none of them could speak English, it was clear that most of them had opinions about me that they were discussing with each other. I was nervous and found their attention a bit overwhelming. So, after a while, I asked Jak if we could go out somewhere to have a coffee.

Mergim came with us to a café in a square near the apartment. He and Jak seemed to have a lot to talk about, but they didn't leave me out of the conversation entirely, and every so often Jak translated for me. 'My cousin thinks you are very beautiful,' he said at one point. 'And that I am very lucky to have you. I told him that he is right.' I could feel myself blushing with pride. In just a few short months, I had gone from being a bullied, miserable, truant schoolgirl to being on the verge of starting a new life in Greece with someone who loved me. I thought I had every reason to feel happy and optimistic. When I look back on it now though, I think the day I arrived in Athens was one of the saddest of my life.

After we had drunk our coffee, Mergim made a phone call. 'He's phoning about a job for you,' Jak told me.

'Where is it?' I asked.

'I don't know yet. But I don't think it's far from here.'

We left the café a few minutes later and walked to a bar where the short, black-haired man who was standing outside the door greeted Mergim and Jak with a handshake. The three men talked for a few minutes, then Jak turned to me and said, 'It looks like you're going to get the job.'

'Aren't I too young to work in a bar?' I asked him. 'I was expecting it to be a café. Don't you have to be 18 to work somewhere like this?'

'No, it's fine,' Jak assured me. 'He knows how old you are, but you look old enough, so it's okay. Don't worry.'

It seemed like an odd way to conduct a job interview; but as I had never had one before, I didn't have any experience to judge it by. And at least the man hadn't taken one look at me and said 'No'.

We went inside and Jak ordered drinks – whisky for himself and Mergim and a coke for me. It was still quite early in the evening and the only other people in the bar were four men and two semi-naked girls pole-dancing on a small wooden stage in the centre of the room. None of them seemed to be taking much notice of each other.

We must have been sitting there for about half an hour when a man came and joined us. He spoke very good English and after he had ordered another round of drinks, he introduced himself to me as the manager of the bar. Then he asked me some questions, including, oddly I thought, 'Do you like dancing?'

'Yes,' I told him, remembering almost wistfully for a moment the dance routines my friend and I used to make up and practise in her garden when we were young. 'But

I've never danced like … that.' I glanced at the two topless girls and felt the heat of a blush suffusing my cheeks.

'Oh, it's easy,' the manager said. 'And don't worry, you won't have to do what they're doing. You'll just do some basic stuff.'

I wasn't sure what he meant by 'basic stuff'. In any case, there was no way I would dance almost naked in a bar. Even the prospect of doing it fully clothed made me feel sick with embarrassed anxiety.

'Well, the job's yours if you want it,' the manager told me. 'I'll leave the three of you to talk it over.'

'I would be much too nervous to dance in front of people,' I told Jak as soon as the man had gone.

'You're going to be brilliant at it,' Jak said, as if it was already a done deal. 'There's no need for you to be nervous: they'll show you exactly what to do. You'll be fine. You're so beautiful.'

I knew what pole-dancing was, of course. I didn't think it was 'wrong' in any way, just weird, and I didn't for one moment link it to sex. Sometimes, I wonder how anyone of almost 15 years old could have been as naïve as I was. I could be stubborn when I had decided I wanted to do something – which was why I had clashed with Mum so often before we left England. In reality, though, I had no self-confidence. And as there was no way I was going to start arguing with Jak and Mergim and then have to tell the manager of the bar that I wasn't going to take the job, I agreed.

'You won't have to do it for long,' Jak said quietly. 'The money's so good we'll have enough for my mum's operation in no time.'

Suddenly I felt like a hero and I knew everything really was going to be okay.

The next morning, Jak took me back to the bar and left me there with the two girls – one Russian, the other African – who were going to teach me to dance in a way that was very different from the dancing I used to do with my friend in her garden back in England! Both girls seemed very confident, although I wondered later if they had been acting, the way I was going to learn to do.

I danced that evening in a dimly lit corner of the bar dressed in an outfit that was really little more than fancy underwear, but that at least covered my boobs. After just a few minutes, another girl took my place. So, although the whole thing was hugely embarrassing, it was mercifully brief and not nearly as bad as it could have been.

The next day, when Jak dropped me at the bar again, the manager said he needed to talk to me. I followed him through a door behind the bar and into a small office, where I stood twisting my fingers nervously as he told me, 'I had complaints about you from customers last night. They pay to see girls dancing topless and if they don't get what they've paid for, I risk being prosecuted for false advertising. You're going to have to dance like the other girls tonight.'

Whether or not what he said was actually true, I felt immediately guilty, as though I had done something wilfully and selfishly wrong. Then I imagined standing on the stage exposing my very flat chest to a roomful of men and I burst into tears.

'I can't do it,' I snivelled. 'And in any case, my boyfriend wouldn't want me to.'

'Oh, don't worry about that. I'll speak to him. He'll be fine with it, I know he will.' He patted my shoulder as if he thought I would be reassured by what he was saying. It was clear that our discussion was now over and I left the room feeling as though I had just been lured into a trap. I was pretty sure Jak wouldn't want me to dance topless in a bar; my overriding concern, however, was the thought of how incredibly humiliating it would be for me.

It turned out that I was wrong about Jak. When I saw him in the bar later that day, he had already spoken to the manager and said that he was okay with the idea of my dancing semi-naked in front of a room full of drunken, lecherous men.

'It will only be for a short time,' he reassured me. 'I don't really want you to stay here and do that. So I'm going to find you another job.'

I tried to tell myself that I was overreacting and that, in the greater scheme of things, getting my kit off was a small sacrifice to make so that Jak's mother's could have the cancer treatment she needed. Jak wasn't doing any gardening jobs now, but he had worked long hours before we came to Athens, for considerably less money than I would be earning. And when I really thought about it, I couldn't justify looking forward to the future we were going to have together while making a fuss about doing something that would help bring it a little bit closer.

Jak stayed at the bar that night, drinking whisky while I danced topless for men whose faces I avoided looking at. And when the manager gave me the 80 euros I had earned, Jak held out his hand and said, 'Why don't you give that to me? I'll look after it for you.'

For the next few nights, Jak and Mergim dropped me off at the bar and then went to a café in a nearby square to wait for me to finish work. When they came back to pick me up, I handed all the money I had earned to Jak. One night, when I kept some of it back because there was something I wanted to buy, his anger really shocked me – until I thought about it and realised I was being selfish and that it was only fair he should take it all, to pay for the food we ate and to save for our future. It was hard-earned money though, because I hated every minute of every night I danced at the bar, and I could never look at the faces of the men who were looking at me.

I had been working there for almost two weeks when Jak told me, 'We've got a meeting tomorrow about another job.'

'Oh, that's great,' I said, feeling as though I had breathed out after holding my breath for just a bit too long. 'What *is* the job?'

'Wait and see,' Jak said.

The next morning, he seemed distracted and barely spoke to me. When I asked him if there was something wrong, he said, 'No. It's okay. Everything's fine.' But he was still quiet and uncommunicative in the taxi that took us to a burger bar in the city centre. Jak led the way up the stairs to the second floor, where the only other customer was a large, overweight man who waved when he saw Jak and then beckoned us over to his table. As we walked towards him, Jak said, 'This is your new boss. He's French and his name's Leon.'

Once the introductions had been made, Leon narrowed his eyes as he looked at me closely for a few seconds and then said something in Greek to Jak. A few minutes later, he leaned forward and passed something under the table, which Jak took and slid into his pocket, although not before I had seen that it was a wad of folded banknotes. I don't think it even crossed my mind to wonder why Leon was giving him money. I didn't understand Greek, so I didn't know what they had been saying to each other. But I trusted Jak. And, after all, he'd had a life before he met me.

'So, you know what you're going to be doing, don't you?' Leon spoke to me in English. 'And you're happy with it?'

I glanced at Jak and he murmured, 'I love you. It's all right.'

'Yes, I'm fine with it,' I told Leon.

I've often wondered what would have happened if I had asked, 'Happy with what? What *is* the job you're offering me?' But I didn't. Jak told me it would be 'all right' and I believed him. So Leon stood up, shook Jak's hand, nodded at me, and then walked down the stairs and out of the restaurant. Jak and I followed him a little while later and took a taxi to another part of the city centre.

On almost every street corner in Athens, there are kiosks selling newspapers and magazines, postcards, sweets, chocolate, cigarettes, even souvenirs and clothes. When we got out of the taxi, Jak told me to wait while he went to one of them. When he came back, he handed me what felt like a flimsy cardboard box in a brown paper bag, pointed to an office building on the other side of the road and said, 'Go up the stairs to the top floor. Knock on the glass door and give this to the guy who opens it.'

'What is it?' I asked him.

'Just *do* it,' he snapped.

Although Jak's anger always took me by surprise and shocked me, I wasn't really frightened of him. But I hated it when he was annoyed with me. So I took the package and turned to cross the road.

'I'll wait for you here,' he called after me, pleasant again now that I was doing what he had wanted me to do.

The woman at the reception desk glanced up when I pushed open the door from the street, and then looked away again as I started to walk up the stairs. The shoes I was wearing had pointed toes and stiletto heels, and long before I had reached the top floor my feet were sore and my legs were shaking. As I stumbled up the last two flights of stairs, I was breathless and, for some reason, had begun to feel uneasy.

The brass plaque on the wall beside the glass doors at the top of the building announced – in both English and Greek – that it was the office of a lawyer. The man who opened the door when I rang the bell was fat and old – at least, he looked old to me.

Snatching the package out of my hands, he told me, in English, to 'Come in and stand over there.' I wished I had the confidence to tell him I had done what I'd been asked to do and now I was going to leave. Instead, I did a sort of nervous side-step across the marble-tiled floor and said nothing.

When he locked the glass doors, I felt a sudden rush of fear. But before I could react in any way, he had opened another door and pushed me through it. In the middle of the small, windowless room he had thrust me into there was a single bed and, at the foot of it, a video camera on a tripod. The only other bit of furniture in the room was a television, playing silently in a corner.

I was so frightened and convinced that he was going to murder me, that I just stood there making little whimpering noises like a defeated and submissive animal. When the man grabbed hold of my vest top and shoved me down on to the bed, I was so shocked my mind went completely blank and I think I barely struggled as he flipped me over on to my back, pulled up my skirt, ripped off my pants and forced himself inside me. The pain was excruciating, but I was too traumatised even to cry.

When he lifted himself off me, I raised my head from the bed and saw the blood. I didn't know it was normal the first time you have sex, and I thought he had done something even more terrible than rape me. And then he did it again.

It was only afterwards, when I was standing beside the bed trying to straighten my skirt, that I realised the soundless scenes playing out on the television were from some horrible, violent porn film. Then the man took a wad of 50-euro notes out of his pocket, thrust them into my hand and told me to get out. 'Go,' he kept saying angrily as he pushed me towards the door – as if I might have some reason to want to stay.

I was still holding my shoes in my hand as I hurried towards the door of the little room. When my toes touched something and sent it skidding across the floor, I glanced down and saw the package Jak had given me, now out of its brown paper bag and lying open, so that I could see the packets of condoms it contained.

I had to hold tightly to the handrail to stop myself falling as I stumbled down the stairs. By the time I had crossed the road outside the office building and thrown myself into Jak's arms, the tears that had been suppressed by shock were streaming down my face.

'What's wrong?' Jak asked. 'Your body is shaking. What's happened?'

'He … I can't …' I stammered.

'Wait.' Jak half-turned towards the street and raised his hand. 'We'll get a taxi and then you can tell me what's happened to upset you so much.'

A few moments later, we were sitting in the back of a taxi, and as it pulled out into the traffic on the busy street, I told him. I was far too shocked and upset to even think about how he would react, but I was completely unprepared for his calm response.

'I'm so sorry,' he said. 'But what we can do? It won't be for long. I love you and you love me. Soon we'll have enough money to start a family and then we'll be together for ever.'

At first, I couldn't understand what he was saying. No one in their right mind would inflict the horrible experience I had just had on anyone, even someone they didn't like. So the idea that Jak *knew* what was going to happen to me when he sent me into the office building simply didn't make any sense. Then I remembered the condoms, and for a moment my certainty wavered. But I knew there had to be some other explanation – because Jak *loved* me.

I didn't even consider the possibility that there might be some link between what had just happened to me and the money Leon had given Jak in the burger restaurant. The part of my brain that normally gathers together fragments of information and combines them into something that makes sense seemed to have shut down. And it was all so far beyond anything I had ever experienced or knew about,

71

it was like a surreal nightmare. So when Jak told me to give him the money, I simply handed him the wad of notes I had been given by the lawyer who had raped me.

'You see!' Jak ran his thumb along the edge of the notes and then flicked through them quickly. 'Already we can start to save for a car. Then we will buy a house. And then …' He patted my knee without looking at me. 'Then we will have somewhere for our children to live.'

I still couldn't see any connection between what he was saying and what had happened to me. Then, suddenly, I understood it, and all the air that should have been flowing into my lungs seemed to have gathered in a solid lump at the back of the throat so that I couldn't breathe. And I was still crying, almost hysterically, when the taxi pulled up outside Jak's cousin's apartment.

'Go and have a shower,' Jak told me, as soon as we got inside. 'Then we'll go out and get something to eat.'

'I'm not hungry,' I said. 'I don't want anything to eat. I want to talk to you. And I want to talk to my mum.' As I said the words, talking to my mum became the only thing in the world that mattered to me.

'Just have a shower,' Jak said again. 'Then we'll work it all out.'

My clothes smelt of the sweat of the man who had stolen my virginity. 'No, not stolen it,' I thought sadly, a sob catching in my throat, 'bought it.' I don't how long I had been standing under the shower, trying to wash all traces of the lawyer off my skin, when I heard Jak calling my name.

'I won't be a minute,' I said, because I knew that however long I stayed in the shower, no amount of soap and water would ever make me clean again.

Jak borrowed his cousin's motorbike and we drove to the other side of the city, down a rocky track beside a beach and then up into the hills. When Jak stopped and turned off the engine, he took hold of my hand, looked into my eyes and said, 'I love you.' But this time I turned away.

'I can't do what you're asking me to do,' I told him. 'There are other ways of earning money. It might take us longer to save the money we need, but that doesn't matter, does it?' While I was speaking, the expression on his face changed to cold indifference and I could feel the muscles in my stomach contracting as I said, 'I need to talk to my mum. Please, Jak, let me phone her. I can't do ... *that*. There *must* be some other way.'

'There is no other way,' he said. 'For God's sake, Megan, stop making such a fuss. I've said I love you and that it'll be all right. What's the matter with you?'

It was as if all my self-disgust and fear had rolled up tightly into a ball of anger and I shouted at him, 'I *want* to speak to my mum. I *won't* do it. I can't believe you're asking me to do something like that.'

What Jak did next took me so much by surprise that I wouldn't have had time to react even if I *had* realised what he was going to do. Jumping to his feet, he grabbed hold of my hair, threw me down on the ground and started kicking me. Instinctively, I curled up into a ball and tried to cover my face with my arms, and he continued to kick my back with so much force it felt as though all the bones in my spine were being smashed. All the time he was attacking me, he was shouting at me in Albanian. Then he bent down, picked up a rock, threw it at me, spat on my prostrate body, swung his leg over the seat of the motorbike and drove away, leaving me lying on the stony ground in a state of physical and mental shock.

The sound of the motorbike's engine had faded into the distance by the time I tried to get up. Every movement made me wince with pain as I crawled to a rock and pulled myself up so that I could sit on it.

'Please come back,' I sobbed into the silence. 'I'm sorry, Jak. Please don't leave me here on my own. Please let everything be all right again.'

What I really wanted though, even more than I wanted Jak to come back for me, was my mum.

Chapter 5

I had no phone, no money and no one to turn to for help except Jak. So all the time I was sitting on the rock, which must have been a couple of hours, I kept telling myself, 'He *will* come back.' The light had begun to fade and it had started getting cold by the time I heard the sound of a motorbike in the distance. Then I told myself instead, 'It will be Jak and not some stranger who'll find me here in the darkness on my own.'

I was so relieved when Jak's motorbike appeared around a bend in the road that I'd have forgiven him for assaulting me even if he hadn't kept saying how sorry he was and that he loved me. 'It's all right,' I told him, a dozen times. And I truly did believe that what had happened must have been my fault.

Despite his apparent remorse, that incident marked a change in Jak's attitude towards me. Looking back on it now, I suppose he had begun the process of breaking me down. Suddenly, it seemed that everything about me was wrong – the clothes I wore, the way I looked, the way I did my hair, the things I said. I became afraid of upsetting him, partly because I was frightened of being physically attacked again and partly because I thought that if I kept getting things wrong, he would leave me. The reality was that I was becoming dependent on him, practically and emotionally. So, mostly, I did whatever he told me to do.

When I was a child and my mother's relationship with John began to fall apart, she became overwhelmed by her own problems. In my early teens, I argued with her about things that didn't matter, because what I believed mattered least of all was me. As I imagine many children do in similar situations, I thought it was my fault my father had left us and that he didn't love me. Now I felt the same way about my relationship with Jak: I believed that when he was angry with me, it was because I wasn't good enough.

Two days after I was raped by the lawyer, Jak and I moved into a hotel and I started working as an escort. For the next six months, we moved from one dingy, cheap hotel to another, and every day I had sex with between six and eight men. Jak always went with me in a taxi to drop me off at their homes or hotel rooms. Then he would wait for me in a café to take me to the next job. I wore the clothes he bought for me and had sex with the men he told me to have sex with. To say I hated it would be a ridiculous understatement. I don't know why I didn't scream and shout and refuse to do it. I think perhaps it was because some part of me that might have resisted it had already started to shrivel up, and it just kept on getting smaller and smaller every day until it disappeared.

It wasn't until after I had started doing the escort work that Jak and I had sex for the first time. He didn't force me to do it with him, but I didn't like it. Maybe becoming a prostitute had made it impossible for me to enjoy having sex with anyone, even the man I still thought I loved. After the first time, he did it with me every morning and every night, even when he was angry with me.

What happened during the daytime was mostly predict-able. What I couldn't ever predict, however, was what sort of mood Jak would be in at night. Sometimes, he would order a takeaway and we'd sit together in whatever dismal hotel room we were staying in and watch a film on the TV. On those occasions, I shut my mind to what I had been doing during the day and felt almost contented. Far more common, however, were the evenings when he'd fly into a rage for no apparent reason and hit me.

He would sometimes humiliate and embarrass me in public, too. For example, one day we were having coffee at a café when I said something that made him angry. Without any warning, he stood up, almost knocking over the table, and poured a jug of water over my head, spat on me and walked away, leaving me sitting there with everyone staring at me.

I hated the way he put my mum down too. He didn't know anything about her, yet he always insisted on telling me that 'No Albanian mother would behave like she does.' Which was pretty rich coming from someone whose mother, I suspect now, didn't have entirely clean hands and who, at the very least, knew about the crimes her son was involved in. I didn't know any of that at the time, though. It just upset me when he talked that way about my mum, because I really loved her. What was almost worse than Jak's criticism, however, was when he said that my mum was sexy and he insisted on describing all the things he would like to do to her, even when I cried and begged him to stop.

Whenever I told him that it really upset me when he talked about my mum like that, he just laughed. I realise now, of course, that it wasn't insensitivity or random unpleasantness that made him do it. Everything he said about my mum was calculated and quite deliberate, because what he was trying to do was drive a wedge between us. If he could separate us – emotionally as well as physically – I would be entirely dependent on him, and therefore much easier to control and manipulate.

I had been doing the escort work for a few weeks when I started feeling ill. Eventually, after I had thrown up a few times, Jak took me to the hospital, where they did a scan and told me I was ten weeks' pregnant. I was ecstatic, particularly when Jak seemed to be pleased about it too. I phoned my mum as soon as we came out of the hospital, and although I could tell she wasn't very happy about the news, I was relieved that she didn't raise the subject of abortion, as I had half-expected her to do. I didn't see being pregnant at 14 as any kind of problem. In fact, quite the opposite, because it would mean that I would be able to stop doing the escort work and then Jak and I, and our children, would live happily ever after.

Although I had two regular clients who didn't use condoms, only Jak ever came inside me. So there was no question about whether the baby was his. Just a few weeks earlier, my mum had been the only person in the world who cared about me at all. Now I had Jak and soon I would have a baby to love and take care of, and to love me too.

That night, Jak phoned his mother, and after he had spoken to her he told me, 'My mum says you shouldn't keep the baby. She thinks it's too early and it will ruin everything.' The bubble of happiness I had been bouncing around in all day had been pricked and I was devastated. I couldn't imagine what it was that his mother thought a baby would ruin – but then I didn't know anything about what Jak was really planning for my future. When I told him how upset I was that his mother had even suggested I should have an abortion, we had a huge row and he stormed out of the hotel, leaving me sitting on the bed crying.

When he came back a couple of hours later, we had something to eat, watched TV and went to bed, without either of us having said very much. Since I had started feeling sick, I had been finding it difficult to sleep at night, so for the last few nights I had slept on a sort of rubber mat on the floor. I lay down on it again that night and after Jak got into the bed we started to talk. I told him I thought the fact that we were going to have a baby should be making us happy and then I tried to explain why I had been upset by what his mother had said. I think that's when we started arguing again.

Suddenly, I couldn't bear it any longer. I got up, went over to the bed and said, 'Please, Jak, don't let's argue.' Then I bent down to hug him, just as his foot shot out from under the bedclothes and he kicked me in the stomach with such force I fell backwards and slid across the tiled floor to the other side of the room. For a moment, I just lay there, slumped against the wall, shocked and bewildered. Then the pain started – somewhere deep in my stomach at first and then spreading like fire throughout my body. I was still leaning against the wall sobbing when Jak turned over and went to sleep.

The next morning, when I started bleeding clots of blood, I was very frightened. Jak took me to the pharmacy and bought me some painkillers for period pains. But although I was in almost constant pain for the next two weeks, he didn't ever suggest I should go to the hospital, and I didn't dare ask him to take me.

I didn't understand that I was having a miscarriage. When I did realise that I had lost the baby, it seemed like a tragedy; whereas, in fact, it was a blessing – certainly for the child, because God knows what would have happened to it if it had been born.

It was a long time before I allowed myself to accept the fact that Jak hadn't simply lashed out at me with his foot in a thoughtless fit of temper. I may not have understood about abortions and miscarriages or about what would really have been involved in having a baby in the situation I was in. I realise now that Jak did, and that he knew exactly what he was doing when he kicked me. By that time, rarely a day passed when he didn't slap me, punch me in the head or drag me around the room by my hair. But he was always careful not to leave marks on any part of my body that could be seen by anyone else. And he never kicked me in the stomach again.

As he systematically took control of every aspect of my life, I was learning to be afraid of him. He would fly into rages, which often seemed to be prompted by jealousy that, even as I became increasingly confused and disorientated, seemed to me to be bizarre in the circumstances. Sometimes, he would ask me about one of the men who had paid to have sex with me that day. 'Tell me what you did with him,' he would say. 'Go on, tell me. You liked it, didn't you?' I wanted to shout that I had *hated* it and that I couldn't bear even to talk about it. But if I didn't answer his questions, he would only get angrier. So I would describe the disgusting, depraved things the man had done to me and then Jak would have sex with me too. And although it was just another ordeal I had to pretend I enjoyed, I did still love him, ridiculous as that sounds when I say it now.

Sometimes he would drop me off at people's houses, but more often I went to hotel rooms. Fortunately, most of the men just wanted 'normal sex' and after they had done it they were almost as keen for me to leave as I was. Some simply wanted company, and some wanted to do things I had had no idea anyone ever wanted to do.

One of my regular clients was a businessman called Andreas who had a nice house in a wealthy part of Athens. He usually booked me for an hour, so Jak would drop me off and then go and wait for me at a café in a nearby square. Andreas didn't ever want sex. Sometimes he would order a takeaway and we would sit and watch TV, and sometimes he would talk to me – in fluent English – about politics and all the other things that interested him. He must have been lonely, but he was kind and cheerful and I got on really well with him and used to look forward to going to his house to see him.

Although Andreas seemed to be the sort of person you might be able to trust, I was wary about what I said to him, in case he repeated it to Jak. I did tell him about Jak though – that he was my boyfriend and that we were going to build a house and start a family. I didn't know how the system of prostitution worked; in fact, I didn't even know there was a system, or that I was part of it. So I told Andreas that I was a 'willing prostitute', working for myself, and he always gave me an extra 50 euros as I was leaving – which I always gave immediately to Jak.

One day, Andreas said he would like to be able to see me without having to go through Leon or Jak first.

'I can't do that,' I told him. 'I would lose my job. And anyway, I love Jak.'

'Well, if you ever do get the chance,' he said, 'if you're ever on your own, come and see me.' He wrote his phone number on a scrap of paper and gave it to me, and before I left his house, I screwed it up into a tiny ball, put it at the bottom of my handbag and prayed that Jak would never find it.

At the opposite end of the spectrum of customers I had at that time was a man who had a whipping fetish. I begged Jak not to make me go back there after the first time, but the guy was paying 1,000 euros an hour. He became a regular client and I saw him at least once every two weeks, always at the same 'love hotel' in the city centre, where people rented rooms by the hour.

He had a big bag, like the sort of thing you'd take to the gym, except that it was stuffed full of whips and canes. Sometimes, he would whip me so hard my skin would feel as though it was on fire and every inch of my back would be covered in swollen, bleeding welts. He would film it all on a video camera that was always set up on a tripod, and when I cried and begged him to stop, he just told me to shut up.

As well as the whipping, he was into anal sex, which was also incredibly painful. When he had finished, he would drag me off the bed and say, 'Get on your knees and open your mouth.' Then he would urinate on my face. I always tried to keep my mouth shut, which was difficult because I was usually crying, and he'd get really angry and shout at me, 'Next time you're going to swallow it.'

If you had any self-esteem, you wouldn't let anyone do that to you. But I already felt like a piece of crap, so it was almost as though I thought being degraded and humiliated was all I deserved. He was another one who spoke good English and I did try to talk to him. I had some idea that if I could make him see me as more than just some object he was filming, he might feel sorry for me. I didn't push it though, because I was afraid of annoying him and getting into really big trouble with Jak. I needn't have worried because he wasn't listening anyway: he wasn't paying a substantial sum of money to hear anything I might have to say. However, he did stop urinating on my face after a while and he didn't whip me quite so hard.

The last time I saw him, I had just had a massive row with Jak. I had a stomach bug, which was making me feel really ill, and when I told Jak I wasn't well enough to go out that day, he flew into a rage and shouted at me, 'You're pathetic. You've got an upset stomach and suddenly you can't cope. I can't decide if the worst thing about you is how weak you are or that you're stupid. Don't you ever think about anyone except yourself? You'll have to go. I need the money.'

Even though I was frightened of Jak by that time, I did sometimes argue with him. I think what made me brave on those occasions was the fact that I still clung to the belief that we were a couple and all the unspeakably horrible things I was doing were for our future together. So perhaps he was right, at least, about my being stupid. What upset me that day was that he had said *he* needed the money, not 'we', although I had just enough sense to know that it wouldn't be a good idea to make a big deal about it. So I got dressed, put on my make-up and went with him in a taxi to the 'love hotel'.

I had been crying silently in the taxi on the way there, and by the time I knocked on the door of the hotel room, I must have looked a bit of a mess. I was sitting on the bed, trying to tidy up my make-up, when the man asked me, 'What's wrong? Has something happened? Tell me what's up.'

There seemed to be genuine sympathy in his voice, and I was feeling very low. So I told him, 'I don't know how I feel about doing this work. I have sex with all these people and it's … it's not really me.' It was a pathetic explanation, particularly in view of what I was actually talking about. But I didn't know any other of way of describing it. What I was doing was something I had never even imagined anyone did, and the way it made me feel was something I couldn't put into words.

The man sat down on the bed beside me and started asking me questions. How many men did I have sex with every day? How much money was I getting? I told him I wasn't getting any money at all. 'My boyfriend keeps it,' I said. Then – not wanting to admit, to either of us, the possibility that Jak might be a bad person – I added quickly, 'But he does pay for all our food, and things like that.'

It sounds crazy now, the idea of sitting in a hotel room and confiding in a man who paid 1,000 euros an hour to film himself whipping me and having anal sex with me. I had hit rock bottom – or thought I had, because I didn't know then that things could get any worse – and it seemed better to have him to talk to than no one at all. And he did seem to be listening to me. So when he started telling me about all his important, influential contacts in the international film industry, I almost dared to believe he was going to offer to help me.

'Do you know what?' he said suddenly, leaning down and taking a gun out of his bag. 'I've lost track of the number of times I've looked at this gun and thought about ending it all.' He turned it over in his hands. 'Is that the way you feel today? Do you feel like you want to end it all?'

A vein in my temple was throbbing and I could taste the sharp taste of vomit. But I forced myself to keep breathing.

'Is that how you feel?' he asked me again. When I still didn't answer, his tone changed and he said angrily, 'I'm asking you a question. Tell me!'

'I suppose I do feel a bit like that,' I whispered. 'But I'd never do it.'

'Hold the gun,' he said, his voice very quiet now. 'Go on, take it.' He put it in my hand. 'It's loaded.'

'No, please, I don't …' My heart was thudding, but when I tried to give the gun back to him, he wouldn't take it.

Suddenly he stood up and shouted, 'Hold it up to your head. No one should have to live like this. Just put the gun to your head, pull the trigger and it will all be over.' I pressed the cold metal of the gun against the side of my head and started to scream. 'Shhh,' he said. 'It's all right. Go on.' And I pulled the trigger.

Before that day, I would have said categorically that I wasn't the sort of person who would ever try to take her own life – whatever sort of person that is. Maybe it was because I'd had a brief, illuminating flash of understanding about what my life with Jak really was and I knew that, whatever I had been telling myself, in reality I had no one. In that split second as I held the gun to my head, aware of nothing except the man's voice telling me how simple it would be to put an end to the terrible mess my life had become, I think I lost my grip on reality.

They say people who've committed suicide have killed themselves 'while the balance of their mind was disturbed'. Maybe, sometimes, they do it during a brief period when they see things clearly and realise it's their only way out. For me, though, it *was* just a passing moment of insanity, so it was very fortunate that the gun wasn't loaded and I didn't blow my own head off in a room in a 'love hotel' in Athens.

After I had pulled the trigger, I dropped the gun on the floor, and I was still sitting on the bed in a state of shock when the man bent down and picked it up. Then he laughed and said, 'You really were going to do it, eh? Is it really that bad? Well, I'm not going to see you anymore. You've obviously got issues.'

Although I didn't realise it until much later, a lot of the jobs I was doing were being set up by the Frenchman, Leon, the man I had met in the burger restaurant who was splitting the proceeds with Jak. For the next few days, I waited in a state of anxious dread for the moment when Jak would find out that the man who had enough money to indulge his fetish for whipping young women had decided to dispense with my services, and would fly into a furious rage. For some reason, it didn't ever happen and he never mentioned the man to me again.

The fact that I had escaped the violent beating I'd antici-pated from Jak did nothing to lessen the indelible mark the incident left on me. I kept thinking about how close I had come to killing myself, and started having flashbacks and nightmares, often waking up in a cold sweat after dream-ing that I had heard the click of the gun's empty cartridge.

I couldn't understand how anyone could do to someone else what that man had done to me; he didn't even know me or have any reason to dislike me. He was right about one thing though: I obviously did have 'issues'. I began to think I wasn't normal, not least because no normal person who didn't actually want to die – as I didn't – would hold a gun to their head and pull the trigger, however much they were coerced and bullied into doing so by someone else.

I was already deeply unhappy and confused before that day; after it, I didn't seem to be able to make sense of anything at all. I kept telling myself that at least I had Jak. But if that was true, why was there a black hole of loneliness inside me that seemed to get bigger every day? The reality was that the only person in the entire world who actually cared about me was my mother, and I was beginning to wonder if I would ever see again.

In fact, it wasn't long after my inadvertent suicide attempt that my mother came back to Greece to live with Nikos, the man who owned the bar where I had first met Jak. While she had been in England, Jak had occasionally let me use his phone to call her. 'Tell her you're working as a waitress,' he'd said. 'And tell her how happy you are.'

'It's really fun,' I told Mum. 'And I'm earning good money. Jak and I are saving up to build our own house. We've got all sorts of plans for the future.' As I said it, I could actually see the house in my head, and imagine how impressed Mum and Nikos would be when they visited us there and saw how well I was taking care of everything.

'As long as you really are happy and Jak's looking after you,' Mum said.

'Oh, he *is*,' I assured her, closing my eyes for a moment and swallowing the lump that had lodged itself in my throat.

Jak had bought me a cheap phone of my own, so that I could call him when I finished jobs, and he let me use it to text and talk to my mum too now that she was back in

Greece. I wasn't allowed to give the number to anyone else – not that I would have had anyone else to give it to. Jak checked the phone every day, just to make sure, and he read all the messages Mum and I sent each other: 'Are you all right?' 'I love you.' 'I can't wait to see you.'

He didn't seem to worry that I might tell her the truth in a phone call. I suppose he was too confident of his own manipulative powers, and perhaps of my gullibility too. And he made sure that I was afraid of Leon, by saying things like, 'You don't want to do anything that would upset him – and, believe me, he *would* find out.'

It might have been true, or it might simply have been a useful way of covering up the fact that it was Jak himself I should have been most afraid of.

Chapter 6

One day, when we had been in Athens for a few months, Jak had a phone call from an Albanian friend of his called Edi who lived in Italy. 'There's a lot of money to be made there,' he told me afterwards. 'Edi suggested we should go out to stay with him for a while and try it out.' I said I didn't want to go, but Jak had already made up his mind.

I didn't really consider the implications of the fact that Jak had a friend in Italy who knew all about the business of prostitution. I think I had given up trying to work out why anything happened. If I had thought about it – or wondered how he knew people like Leon – I might have come to the conclusion that even before he met me, Jak had known something about prostitution too, and that he hadn't got me involved in it by chance.

Edi met us off the ferry in Italy a couple of days later and that night he took us out in his car to show me the road where I would be working. I knew some basic Greek by that time and understood more or less how things worked in Greece. So I had been dreading starting again in a country where I didn't speak or understand the language at all. What I hadn't realised was that I would be working outside.

'I don't want to stand on the street,' I told Jak and Edi, my voice shrill with panic. 'Can't I do escorting?' A few weeks earlier, I had been appalled and terrified by the thought of escorting; now it seemed to be very much the lesser of two evils.

'You'll be fine,' Edi said, as if he was reassuring an unnecessarily anxious, fretful child.

There were times – like this one – when I felt as though I had become trapped inside someone else's life. I was like a character in a film who's been mistaken for another character and decides, for plot-related reasons, to go along with it and pretend they really are that person. I had been mistaken for a prostitute, but it would all get sorted out in the end, as long as I held on to the memory of who I really was. The problem was, though, that Jak seemed to have forgotten that I wasn't really a prostitute, and that sometimes made it difficult for me to be certain about my true identity. It was a problem I thought would only be made worse by having to stand on a street corner waiting to be picked up by any stranger who wanted to have sex with me.

That night, Edi drove down a long, dimly lit road where dozens of girls and transsexuals were already in their places ready for the night's work that lay ahead of them. He stopped the car a short distance past where the last girl was standing, just beyond the arc of light cast by the final streetlight, and said, 'This is where you'll be working tomorrow night. We'll be parked over there.' He pointed to somewhere in the darkness on the other side of the road. 'We'll be able to see what's going on, and we'll follow every car you get into.'

'I can't do it,' I whispered, but neither he nor Jak seemed to hear me.

The next morning, the two men took me out and bought me a short skirt, a belly top with a halter neck and a pair of high-stiletto-heeled shoes. They were the sort of shiny, cheap clothes people might imagine a hooker would wear, and quite different from the more subdued, almost childish clothes Jak had previously bought for me. Just as it was starting to get dark, I did my hair and make-up, Jak put glittery gel all over my body, and then Edi drove us back to the street where the prostitutes were already gathering.

Before they dropped me off, Edi slowed down as he passed two large trees separated by a patch of grass on the opposite side of the road from 'my spot'. 'That's where we'll be parked,' he said. 'As long as you stay where I showed you, we'll be able to see you from there. So you'll be perfectly safe.'

There wasn't any part of what I was about to do that would be 'perfectly safe'. Even someone as naïve and apparently willing to lie to themselves as I was could see that. Once again, I don't know why I didn't simply say, 'I'm not going to do it.' When I had some counselling a little while ago, the therapist talked about learned behaviour, dependency and all the other complicated characteristics that might make some people identifiable to traffickers as potential victims. If you add fear of violence to all those other factors, I suppose you arrive at some sort of explanation.

I didn't speak any Italian, but Edi had told me what to say, and when I was standing at the side of the road, shivering and feeling sick, I kept going over the unfamiliar words in my head. When the first car pulled up beside me, I must have managed to say something that made sense, because a few seconds later I was sitting in the passenger seat, praying silently that Jak and Edi had seen me get into the car and weren't far behind us. As the guy drove down the road looking for somewhere to stop, I had to fight the urge to turn round and see if they were there. Then I caught sight of Edi's car reflected in the wing mirror and almost cried with relief.

The first man wanted oral sex, as most of the others did. I hated doing it. But at least it was quick, and within minutes I was standing in the cold darkness at the side of the road again, waiting to be picked up by someone else.

I earned between 2,000 and 2,500 euros a night, every night for two weeks. Jak and Edi drove past me at intervals to collect the money – so that I wasn't mugged, they said. The rest of the time, they did what they had promised they would do, and watched me from a distance. Fortunately, no one ever did try to hurt me. Perhaps what helped to dissuade them was the fact that as soon as I got into a car I always said that people were following us to make sure I was safe. Even so, the possibility was always there with every new encounter.

When I finished work in the early hours one morning, Jak and Edi had picked me up as usual and we drove to a petrol station, where Edi filled up the car. He had just got back behind the steering wheel when a police car pulled in behind us. One of the two policemen who got out of it walked around our car to the driver's side and knocked on the window. 'Don't speak. Don't say anything,' Jak said to me over his shoulder.

The policeman told Edi and Jak to get out of the car and then asked to see their documents. I kept very still, hoping he wouldn't notice me on the back seat, but while he was checking their papers, the other policeman flashed the beam of his torch around the inside of the car and directly into my face. I closed my eyes and turned away from the blinding light. When I opened them again, his colleague was handing the papers back to Jak and Edi and saying, in English, 'Go. And don't let us see you here again. If you come back, we will arrest you. Do you understand?'

The next day, Jak told me we were leaving. 'It's too risky here,' he said, 'and we're not making any more money than we do in Athens.' A couple of hours later, we were on the ferry again, on our way back to Athens.

I didn't know anything about the laws related to prostitution at that time, but although prostitution itself is legal in Italy, organised prostitution, controlled by a third party, is not. In Greece, on the other hand, more or less anything is legal, in brothels, on the street, pimping – although not for anyone under the age of 21, as I was.

A few days after we had returned from Italy, Jak had another meeting with Leon, and I went with him to a burger restaurant in a different city square. There was a man with Leon this time, a Romanian who he introduced as Elek. I sat drinking my coffee while the three men talked to each other in a language I didn't recognise. Then Leon turned to me and said, 'We're talking about a special anal job you're going to do tonight.'

I glanced anxiously at Jak, who just shrugged and said, 'I know you hate doing anal, but the guy's old and can't really get it up anyway. So it won't hurt and …'

'And it's worth two thousand euros,' Leon interrupted him. 'So don't fuck it up.' He cracked his knuckles, then looked at his watch and added, 'I think we've just got time for another coffee.'

The money wasn't going to benefit me in any way, so it was odd how mentioning it made me feel the pressure of responsibility. It was similar to the way I'd felt when I had shoplifted in England: I hadn't wanted to do it, but when my friend said, 'Come on, quick; do it now,' it had seemed as though I didn't have a choice. As far as the three men were concerned, the matter was already decided. And then it dawned on me with sickening clarity that there must be something they weren't telling me: 2,000 euros was a lot of money to pay for anal sex, whatever the state of virility of the old man. Even the guy with the whips, video camera and gun had only paid 1,000. I wanted to tell Jak I was frightened and beg him not to make me do it. When I saw the cold warning in his eyes, I asked instead, 'How long will I have to stay?'

'It's just normal, about an hour, maybe less.' Leon shrugged.

Elek's tone was kinder though, as he said, 'Don't be nervous. You'll be fine. Do you speak any Greek?'

'A bit,' I told him. In fact, I had been surprised by how quickly I picked it up during the months I had been in Athens, particularly when few of the people I came into contact with had any interest in talking to me.

'Well, make sure they don't realise that when you go to this job tonight,' Elek said. 'As far as this guy is concerned, you're an English tourist on your first visit to Greece. That's what you say if anyone asks you, okay?'

After we had drunk our coffee, Elek turned to me again and said, 'I'm going to be taking over from Leon for a while. I'll be finding you jobs from now on, and meeting up with you and Jak from time to time.' He took my phone and put his number into it. 'In fact, I'm going to take you to the place today.' A few minutes later, I was sitting on the back of his motorcycle on the way to do a job I was dreading more than I had dreaded any of the ones I'd done so far.

Elek stopped outside an apartment building in an area of the city where a lot of wealthy bankers, politicians and high-ranking government officials lived. 'Right,' he said. 'This is what's going to happen. When you get inside, a woman will be there to meet you. She'll put a blindfold over your eyes and …'

Suddenly I knew why the man was willing to pay so much money: the only possible explanation was that I was going to be murdered. 'I don't want to do it,' I whimpered.

'What do you mean you don't want to do it?' Elek's earlier friendliness had been replaced by terse anger. 'You've got no choice now. You can't just change your mind. These are important people, you know; they haven't got time to waste.' He took out his phone, dialled a number and said in English, 'We're here, at the gates.' One of the security cameras above the wrought-iron railings moved almost imperceptibly, then there was a buzzing sound from the gate and Elek pushed it open, saying as he did so, 'Don't worry. It'll be fine. Phone me when you're ready to leave and I'll be here to pick you up.'

I was just stepping into the courtyard when his phone rang. He reached out to catch the gate with his hand and told me to wait while he answered it, and after listening for a moment he said, 'I'm going to have to come with you.'

A woman with short grey hair and a sour expression met us just inside the apartment block and handed Elek a fat envelope, which he slipped into an inside pocket of his jacket. Then he turned and walked away. I knew it must be the 2,000 euros. But why pay it to Elek in advance? People usually gave the money to me when I did escort jobs. It seemed to be further proof that something really bad was going to happen to me, something that would prevent me being able to leave with the money myself. It did cross my mind to start screaming. There must have been people in some of the apartments who would have heard me and, at the very least, would have opened their doors to see what was happening. But, for some reason, the fact that the money had already been paid made me think that wasn't an option.

After Elek had gone, the woman took a strip of material out of the pocket of her dress and indicated for me to turn round. Then she placed a blindfold over my eyes and tied it behind my head. I was shaking and had begun to cry when I asked her, 'Why are you doing this? Why do I have to wear a blindfold?'

'Because this man is well known,' she answered, in heavily accented English. 'You must not see this man.'

For a moment, I had a strange sense of calm, as though my mind had given up and simply accepted the fact that if they really were planning to kill me, there was nothing I could do about it now. It didn't last long though. I'm not the sort of person who is struck dumb by fear; panic makes me voluble, and I was sobbing loudly as the woman tightened the blindfold and checked to make sure I couldn't see. Then she took hold of my arm and led me down the marble-floored corridor, telling me sharply to, 'Stop crying! Shut up! Stop now!' When I stumbled, she clicked her tongue irritably and then put her arm around my waist to support me.

'Please tell me what's going to happen to me,' I sobbed. 'You're going to kill me, aren't you? Please tell me if you are. I need to know. I'm from England and I just want to go home.'

The woman gave a snort of laughter and said scornfully, 'No one's going to kill you! But if you don't shut up, he'll tell you to leave, and then you'll be in trouble.'

I realised we must have entered a room when the sound of our footsteps changed, and when the woman said something in Greek, a man's voice answered. Suddenly I began to shout, 'No! I don't have to do this. You're going to hurt me. They said I didn't have to do it.' As my panic tipped over into hysteria, I would have said anything, told any lie to stop them doing what I knew they were going to do.

'Be calm.' The woman's voice was quiet and kinder than it had been before. 'It's all right. Don't worry. Just take off your skirt and pants.'

Still whimpering, I had started tugging at my clothes when I heard noises behind me that made me freeze. It sounded like a drawer being opened and closed and then metal tapping against metal. The fear was like a solid weight pressing on my chest, crushing all the air out of my lungs and blocking my throat so that I couldn't swallow. I was still struggling to breathe when I was pushed face-down on to the bed and heard the woman say, in Greek, 'Okay? I'll get it ready.'

'Get what ready?' I shrieked, forgetting what Elek had told me about not letting them know I could understand or speak the language.

For a moment, no one said anything; then a man's voice asked, 'Do you speak Greek?' When I didn't answer, he asked the question again, this time in English.

'No,' I said. 'No, I … I just know one or two words.' And then my first coherent thought struck me: if it was so important to them that I didn't speak Greek, perhaps it was something I could use to try to save myself. I started shout-ing, 'Yes, I *do* speak Greek. I can understand everything you're saying. So you'd better not hurt me.' But my defiance was short-lived, and I was crying again as I begged them, 'Please, don't hurt me.'

'We're not going to hurt you,' the man said. Then, speak-ing to the woman in Greek again, he asked, 'What are we going to do now?'

'Shall we take the blindfold off?' she said. 'Maybe if it calms her down …'

'No!' The man's tone was emphatic. 'Definitely not! I don't trust this girl.'

I think the woman was hoping to calm me down when she said, 'It's all right. I'm just going to clean you out.' In

101

fact, her words had the opposite effect and I started shouting, 'What do you mean? What are you doing?' In some ways, it might have been better not to have asked, because what she described to me was some sort of colonic irrigation involving a length of tubing and a pump. It was horrible, but fear is tiring and by that point I just wanted to get it all over with as quickly as possible.

I had already sensed that the man was standing behind me before he spoke. 'I don't get very hard,' he said. 'And I come very quickly. So I won't hurt you.' It did hurt though and by the time he had finished I was crying and begging him to stop.

A few minutes later, the woman led me back down the marble corridor, removed the blindfold, pressed a button to open the gate and let me out.

As I stepped out on to the street into the sunshine, I felt disorientated in the way you do when you come out of a cinema after seeing a film in the daytime. I was anxious too, because I thought the man would tell Elek I had made a fuss and then he would tell Jak and I'd get into really bad trouble.

For the next couple of days, I kept expecting Jak to start shouting at me, but he never did – at least, not about the wealthy man who liked anal sex and didn't want to be identified. Perhaps, if the man was someone who was well known in Greece, he didn't want to make a fuss about what had happened and risk upsetting the people who supplied him with foreign girls to gratify his weird sexual appetites.

I was working seven days a week, doing between eight and twelve jobs a day, each of which lasted for anything from a few minutes to an hour. Jak and I got up at six o'clock every morning and were out of the hotel by nine at the latest. He took me to all the jobs, in people's homes and in offices, and then back to the hotel. It was a routine that became my life, without my understanding how or why. If you have very low self-esteem and no confidence, you tend to accept other people's evaluation of your worth, and it didn't cross my mind that I might deserve better.

One of my regular clients was an optician. He would usually be shutting up shop when Jak dropped me off. On the occasions when he did still have someone with him, he would say to me quite casually, as if I was just another customer, 'Hi. How are you? Just give me five minutes please and I'll be with you.' And I would sit down to wait for him, feeling embarrassed and wondering if the person trying on frames for their new glasses knew why I was really there. When the customer had gone, he would close the shop, pull down the shutters and we would either go into a tiny back room or he would take me to an empty apartment just around the corner.

The optician was one of a few men who didn't use condoms. I dreaded doing it that way, but Jak told me it was okay because both he and Leon – and later Elek – always checked their health papers and made sure that they were clean. Even though I chose to believe him, despite the fact that I knew it cost the men more to do it without a condom, I still worried about it.

I was in the shop with the optician one day when his wife and children turned up. The shutters were down so she couldn't see us. But when she kept ringing the bell, I was sure she must know we were in there. It was horrible. I felt terrible, as though what was happening was *my* fault rather than the fault of the man who was cheating on his wife by having sex with a prostitute. I was scared too, and used to dread going there after that.

There were lots of things I didn't know about sex before I went to Greece. One of them was that there are men who derive sexual pleasure from inflicting pain on women. I came across quite a few men like that while I was there, as well as some who frightened me for other reasons.

Jak took me to do an escorting job one day at a dilapidated old house that was set slightly apart from its neighbours at the end of a dark street. I told him as he was dropping me off, 'I've got a really sick feeling about this place. I think there's something wrong here.'

'Well, you've got your phone,' he said. 'If you feel as though you're in any danger, you can speed dial me and I'll come straight back. I'm not going far. I'll be waiting for you in a café just round the corner.'

Perhaps the fact that I felt grateful to him for those few words of comfort is an indication of how distorted normality had become for me. Despite his reassurances, however, I felt very nervous as I walked up the path and rang the bell on what appeared to be a metal front door. The guy who opened it was probably in his mid-forties, with greasy hair, stained clothes and long, dirty fingernails.

When he led the way into a room that stank of vomit and stale sweat, I had to force myself to sit down on the grimy, threadbare sofa. Then he just stood there in front of me, laughing and making weird twitching movements with his head, and it felt as though hundreds of tiny insects were crawling all over my skin. I was so unnerved by him that I had already begun to move my hand, very slowly, towards the pocket where I'd put my mobile phone, when two very bad things happened almost simultaneously. The first was that I suddenly remembered that I had transferred the phone from my pocket to my handbag as Jak and I were leaving the hotel. The second was that I noticed an axe propped up against the wall a few feet away from where the man was standing.

'I'm sorry,' I said in Greek. 'I … I'm afraid I feel sick. So … I'm just going to go.' I opened my handbag as I was speaking and began, surreptitiously and blindly, to search for my phone. 'My boyfriend's waiting for me outside. I'm going to phone him and tell him I'm leaving your house now.' I tried to sound confident, but he must have been able to hear the panic in my voice. He stared at me almost blankly for a second, as if he was trying to remember who I was and why I was in his house. Then he said, very loudly, in English, 'No! Do not move.'

The sound of his voice had almost the same effect as a physical blow and I burst into tears, pleading with him like a little girl, 'Please, don't hurt me. I know you're going to hurt me. Please don't.'

'I am going to hurt you.' He repeated the words several times, very slowly, as if he was examining them one by one in his mind.

'What *are* you going to do to me?' I whispered, not because I really wanted to know, but because some instinct was prompting me to try to make him talk to me. I think I hoped that it might make him see me as a human being, or maybe I was simply trying to buy myself some time. Stupidly though, I let my eyes return to the axe. The man glanced sideways to see what I was looking at, and then, in what seemed to be just one swift movement, snatched it up and held its mud-caked blade against my throat.

As the cold steel touched my skin, I threw up. The man dropped the axe on the floor at his feet and started to laugh. Grabbing the opportunity while he was distracted, I reached into my bag, pulled out my phone and pressed Jak's number on speed dial. Mercifully, Jak answered almost immediately and as soon as I heard his voice I blurted out, 'I can't do this. I need to get out of here right now.'

'Ah, don't go.' The man leered at me, displaying a mouthful of uneven, nicotine-stained teeth. 'I was only joking.'

Clutching my bag to my chest like a shield, I jumped up and ran to the front door. I was still struggling to open it when I felt his arm touch the side of my body. When I tried to scream, no sound came out. Then, through the blinding haze of my panic, I realised that he had opened the door for me and was letting me go.

My heart was thudding as I ran down the path and out on to the street. I had hoped to find Jak already there and waiting for me, but there was no sign of him. I phoned him again, glancing round me all the time as I did so, expecting the man to come after me. But he didn't follow me and a few minutes later I was sitting on the back of Jak's motorcycle, crying silently and thinking, with desperate longing, about my mother.

I thought Jak would sympathise and say how sorry he was that I'd had to go through such a horrible ordeal. So I was completely taken aback when he closed the door of our hotel room and started shouting at me for messing up 'such a simple job'.

'But the man had an axe,' I told him, angry now as well as hurt by his reaction. 'I thought you would be relieved that I hadn't come to any harm.'

Jak's first punch literally lifted me off the ground and sent me flying across the room. I was still lying on the floor, dazed and shocked, when he twisted his fingers in my hair, dragged me to my feet and banged my head repeatedly against the wall. Then he thrust his fingers between my teeth and lifted me off the floor, scraping his nails along the roof of my mouth as he did so. It felt as though every part of the inside of my mouth was swelling up, blocking my throat and making me choke. The pain was excruciating and I had the metallic taste of blood in my mouth. I had never seen him in such a furious rage. While I was gasping for breath, he kept on punching me, and each blow sent my head crashing back against the wall. When he finally let go of me, darkness rushed in and I crumpled on to the floor at his feet.

I think I must have lost consciousness for a moment, because the next thing I remember is hearing Jak shouting into the phone, 'Help! You have to help me. I think I might have killed her.' When I opened my eyes again, Jak and the Albanian owner of the hotel were looking down at me.

I had learned quite a bit of Albanian from Jak by that time, although the barely controlled panic in both men's voices would have been recognisable in any language. The hotel owner kept swearing and saying angrily, 'You stupid idiot! What have you done to her?' I think he was the one who slid his arm underneath me to lift my head and shoulders off the floor and then put two broad, rough-skinned fingers into my mouth until they were touching the back of my throat. For a moment the pain was so intense I thought I was going to pass out. Then my whole body convulsed and, for the second time that evening, I threw up.

Jak made me stay in bed for the next couple of days – although, in fact, I didn't need any persuasion. The inside of my mouth was so swollen and sore I could barely swallow, and I had a relentless headache that was, almost literally, blinding. When Jak sat beside me, trying to feed me soup, he apologised over and over again for what he had done. 'Sometimes I can't control my anger,' he said. 'You know that my family has always lived in poverty: that's where the rage comes from. I get angry when I think that my parents have nothing. And sometimes I take it out on you. But it won't happen again, I promise.'

Apart from some bruising around my mouth, I had almost no visible marks anywhere on my body as a result of Jak's assault. I didn't realise it until much later, but that wasn't accidental. Although he was often physically violent with me after that day, he never did actually lose control, despite often appearing to do so, and he was always very careful not to cut or bruise any part of me that would be seen by someone else.

This time, like every subsequent time he attacked me, he managed to convince me that it would never happen again. And this time, like every subsequent time he attacked me, I believed him. I think part of the reason why I allowed myself to be persuaded that he really was full of remorse was because I had seen him panic when he thought he had really hurt me. I mistook his reaction for concern about me, rather than realising that the only person he was ever concerned for was himself. It was a very long time before I accepted the fact that what upset Jak – and the hotel owner – so much that day when he thought he had killed me was the prospect of having to dispose of my body without anyone finding out what he had done.

I had been in Athens with Jak for about six months by that time. I don't think my teachers back in England, or the policeman who had picked me up for shoplifting, would have recognised the emaciated, timid girl with a trance-like expression and dark rings under her eyes as the same mouthy, stubborn teenager they'd had to deal with less than a year earlier. The only strong emotion I ever really felt now was fear, and even that seemed to fade almost as quickly as it came.

Without being consciously aware that it had happened, I had accepted the fact that I no longer controlled any aspect of my life. In a way, that made things less compli-cated, because if there wasn't anything I could do to change the course of events, there was no point trying – and trying would have involved the use of physical and mental energy I simply didn't have.

What I did need to concentrate on was learning how to separate my mind from my body. I knew instinctively that it was the only way I would manage to survive being regu-larly assaulted by men whose depraved sexual appetites made them unable to empathise with me or even see me as another human being.

In time, the thought of dying became less frightening too: it doesn't seem like such a big deal when you're living a life that couldn't possibly get any worse. At least, that's what I thought then. But I was wrong. Nothing could have prepared me for how bad my life was about to become.

Chapter 7

When I was in England, I used to dread getting my period. It always lasted for at least a week and was really painful. Even in Greece it was so bad that Jak used to give me the time off. I looked forward to those few days every month when we would do things together that normal couples do – except that when we went out shopping, it was only Jak that would be buying clothes and often gold for himself. He had a lot of money to spend, because I earned well over 1,000 euros almost every day for the rest of the month, plus tips, which I used to give him too. There was no question of trying to hide anything from him, because he checked my phone and went through my bag regularly.

I believed Jak when he told me he had been brought up in poverty, so although I was earning the money by doing something I desperately didn't want to do, I was happy when he bought himself expensive clothes. He would often say to me, 'One day, we're going to eat the best meat. One day, we'll be rich.' And I would feel pleased that he was pleased. It makes me very sad when I think about that now.

On the days when I had my period we would also go to cafés and eat in fast-food restaurants. I only ever held money in my hand for as long as it took me to walk out of a client's house or hotel room and give it to Jak. Consequently, he paid for everything, which I interpreted as a sign that he really did love me. (You can see signs of anything anywhere if you look hard enough for them.) After I had been in Greece for a while, my periods got a lot better, but I didn't tell Jak. I pretended they were as bad as they had always been. In fact, I would sometimes exaggerate how much they hurt and how long they lasted, just so I didn't lose those precious days off.

After the day when I ran away from the man with the axe and Jak punched me and sent me flying across the room, he was often violent towards me. Surprisingly, perhaps, I did sometimes try to stand up to him. Occasionally when he shouted at me, I would shout back and we'd have a loud, angry argument. I wasn't being brave; I think I did it because I couldn't bring myself to accept that we weren't 'in a relationship'. If I'd had to admit that, there wouldn't have been one single thing to make my life worth living.

If Jak got into a rage with me when we were out, he would sometimes just walk away and leave me stranded in the street. I didn't have any money, so I couldn't get a taxi, and there were times when I would have to walk a long way to find whatever hotel we were staying in. I suppose the strangest thing of all is the fact that I always *did* go back to the hotel. But Jak and Leon often warned me about what would happen if I ever went to the police, and because I had no reason not to believe them, running away simply didn't seem to be an option. I suppose it was like any other relationship with a violent partner – based partly on fear, partly on the belief that every time they hit you it's actually your fault. Logically, it doesn't make any sense not to leave someone the first time they raise their hand to you, or to stay with a man who's making you do the things I was doing. I really did think I was to blame every time Jak was angry and, absurd as it sounds, I did still love him.

What I didn't realise at the time was that none of Jak's reactions was a genuine, spur-of-the-moment response. His anger, tears of regret or self-pity, praise and affection were all equally contrived. He wasn't emotionally volatile, as he always claimed to be; he was cold, calculating and very clever. Everything he said and did was part of the process of deliberately distorting my sense of reality and brainwashing me. Even before I went to Athens, when I was getting into trouble and truanting from school, I didn't really know who I was or who I wanted to be. After just a few months with Jak, the answer seemed to be 'nobody'.

Jak controlled not just the money, but also every aspect of my life. While we were out buying expensive clothes for him, he would occasionally buy a cheap outfit for me. He never got me short skirts or revealing tops, or anything else you might imagine a prostitute would wear; he always bought clothes that made me look young. Every day, he would lay out what he wanted me to wear and sometimes he would tell me to do my hair in pigtails. I think he often sold me as a little girl – an even younger little girl than I actually was. Some of the men had their own ideas about what schoolgirls should be wearing, and I would put on the clothes they brought for me, things like school uniforms with very short skirts, stockings and high heels.

One man, called Thanos, was absolutely obsessed by porn – just the 'normal' stuff fortunately, not anything *really* horrible. He would book me every week for four or five hours, always in a hotel room, and take pictures of me wearing leather outfits or weird knickers with zips or, more often, of me naked in all sorts of pornographic poses. He was very polite, but it was obvious the first time he spoke to me that there was something peculiar about him. He was like an incredibly fussy film director. He would give me precise instructions about how to lie and how to position my arms and legs, then he'd adjust everything repeatedly, making me move an inch this way or that way until he was happy with every last detail and finally ready to take his photograph.

Sometimes he would tie me up, take his photographs and then have sex with me. Being photographed was humiliating enough, especially for someone as shy as I was. The sex was far worse: it would go on for hours and it always hurt so much I would be crying while he was doing it. I would try to make sure he could see I was crying, because I wanted him to know he was hurting me, but he didn't give a crap; he didn't care about me at all. It was horrible. What sort of person gets a kick out of doing something to someone who's clearly distressed and in pain? It makes me so angry, even now. I came across a lot of men who were like Thanos in one way or another. I still can't understand how they function in the normal world when there's so obviously something seriously wrong with them.

One night, after we had been in Athens for about six months, Jak said, 'I'm going home tomorrow.' I never knew what would annoy him and set him off, so although I felt like jumping up and hugging him, I kept my excitement under control as I asked, 'What do you mean? Are we going back to the coast, to your parents' house?'

'*I* am going home, yes,' he said. 'But you have to stay here.'

It was like being punched. During the last six months, I had lost everything except Jak; and now I was going to lose him too. I didn't even think to argue or to say that I didn't want to continue working as a prostitute. My immediate concerns were about practical issues. Who would drop me off at clients' houses and hotels if Jak wasn't there to do it? Who would wait for me somewhere nearby in case I needed help? Would I be expected to take care of everything on my own? Who would look after the money?

What I actually asked was, 'How long will you be gone? What will happen to me?'

'You'll be fine,' Jak said. 'Elek will look after you.'

I cried when Jak left the hotel the next morning. 'I'll be back,' he assured me. 'Until I am, I'll keep in touch by phone. And remember what I told you about the money: you give half of everything you earn to Elek and once a week you send the other to me by Western Union. For fuck's sake, stop snivelling for a minute and listen to me. Do you understand what I'm telling you? It's really important.'

'Yes, I understand,' I said, although really I didn't, because I believed he was going to save the money I would be sending him for our future together.

Some teenage girls are level headed, sensible, confident and emotionally well balanced; others are naïve, gullible, easily frightened and emotionally needy. Girls in the second of those two broad categories are the ones who become victims of sex traffickers and internet grooming, and who get themselves into the sort of colossal mess I was in. They're the ones who can be bullied and coerced into doing things that will scar them for the rest of their lives. They're the ones who can be persuaded that almost anything and everything is their fault, and that they're 'not good enough' in all sorts of important ways. Whereas the truth is that people who buy and sell other human beings are clever, manipulative, self-serving, totally devoid of any normal feelings, and have no compassion for the 'commodities' they trade in. People like Jak don't do anything random: they're running a business, and that's what informs every single decision they make.

Everyone's view of the world and of what happens to them and to other people is based on their own experiences. Partly because of my childhood experiences, I still want to believe that Jak loved me – even just a little bit, at some time. If I accept that he didn't, I have to consider the possibility that I'm not lovable, and that maybe that's why my father didn't care about me, and why sometimes when I was a child it seemed that my mother didn't either. The logical part of my brain tells me that my parents behaved the way they did for reasons that had nothing to do with me and that they had complicated emotional issues of their own, perhaps because of things that happened to *them* in *their* childhood. But even though I know all that, I still find myself wondering sometimes when I'm feeling really low if it's the whole truth.

Jak was very good at making me believe that what happened to me was my fault. The fact is, though, that he chose me quite deliberately as his victim because I was very young and because he could tell that I was naïve, vulnerable and emotionally a bit screwed up. Human traffickers don't prey on people who are confident, whose life experiences have been more positive than negative and who are likely to fight back.

When Jak left me that morning in the horrible, cockroach-infested hotel room, I was distraught. I was still lying on the bed crying when the phone in the room rang. When I answered it, the Albanian hotel owner said, 'Get yourself ready and be downstairs in the bar in 15 minutes.'

I didn't get a chance to ask him, 'Get ready for what?' I had no idea what was going to happen next; I was like a little dog waiting for its master to tell it what to do. Fifteen minutes later, I had washed my tear-stained face, put on some make-up and was downstairs, sitting at one of the tables in the bar. The hotel owner was already there, drinking whisky, and he called across the room to ask me if I wanted a drink.

'No thanks,' I said. 'I'm fine.'

'Elek will be here soon. Why don't you have a drink while you're waiting for him?' he persisted. And because I didn't want to offend or annoy him, I relented and asked for some water. 'Not water!' He sounded scornful. 'Have a proper drink.'

'No thanks, I don't really like alcohol,' I said. 'Water will be fine.' But he was already pouring whisky into a glass, which he put down on the table in front of me, saying almost aggressively, 'Come on, try this.'

'I said I wanted water.' I tried to sound confident so that he wouldn't know I was suddenly feeling anxious. 'Just because my boyfriend has gone doesn't mean you can tell me what to do.'

'Drink it!' The hotel owner slammed his fist down on the table with such force that a crack appeared on its surface.

After I had drunk the whole glass of whisky in one mouthful, a warm glow seemed to spread through my body. The man laughed and asked if I wanted another one, and this time when I said no, he shrugged his shoulders and said, 'Okay, later then. Later, you and me will have a drink together.'

When Elek arrived at the hotel, he came into the bar, sat down beside me and said, 'The escorting work is dying down. We're going to have to go to the next level.'

'What do you mean?' I asked, anxiety rippling like waves through my body. 'What next level?'

Elek always spoke to me in either English or Greek, but as I didn't know the word 'bordello' in either language, I didn't understand when he told me that that's where I would be working. When I asked him what it was, he said, 'It's like … It's inside sex.'

'Inside what?' I felt sick. Surely there couldn't be any perverted sexual acts I didn't already know about. I was almost relieved when Elek said, 'Working in a bordello is like working inside a house. I'll pick you up tonight. This work is very tiring, so to begin with you'll be in one of the less busy places.' Even then, I don't think I really understood that a 'bordello' was a brothel.

After Elek left, I went upstairs to my room and waited. He phoned me several times during the afternoon and then came back for me on his motorbike in the early evening and drove to the centre of Athens. The small stone house he stopped outside was almost identical to all the other houses in the long narrow street, most of which had coloured lamps hanging next to their metal front doors.

I had never been inside a brothel before, and the ones I'd seen in films were nothing like the cold, damp room I was taken into, which was lit by disco lights and stank of sweat and stale alcohol. Elek introduced me to the brothel owner, a huge, grubby-looking woman who reminded me of Agatha Trunchbull in the film *Matilda*. Then he gave me a small box with '250 Condoms' written on the side of it and said, 'You'll need these.' I began to panic. Why would I need so many? How long was Elek going to leave me there? Doing the escorting work, I usually had around 8 clients a day, and I was still trying to divide 250 by 8 when Elek handed me some clothes and told me to go and put them on.

'You look really good,' he said a few minutes later, when I was standing in front of him wearing a tight black vest decorated with tiny red roses, a matching frilly thong and a pair of stiletto-heeled shoes. 'You're going to do well tonight.' I must have looked as anxiously miserable as I felt, because he laughed as he added, 'Don't worry. It's much better to be here than doing what you're used to doing. It's a lot quicker. You don't have to talk to the men. You don't let them touch you and you don't let them do *anything* without condoms, not even for extra money. All you have to do is open your legs, they fuck you, and then they leave. It really is as simple as that!'

Maybe it did seem simple to him. Maybe to a man who had control over his own life and didn't consider a girl like me to have anything at all in common with, say, his mother or his sister, it did seem to be merely a job. To me though, working in a brothel was a very frightening, soul-destroying prospect, and probably the worst thing I could ever have imagined myself doing.

After Elek left, the woman told me, 'We open in half an hour. Your hair looks a mess. Go and sort it out, and then do your make-up. You need a lot more make-up than you're wearing.' When she was satisfied with the way I looked, she took a handful of condoms out of the box Elek had given me and laid them out in rows on a table, four in the first row and several rows of ten underneath it. Then she handed me a piece of paper and a pencil and said, 'Everyone pays twenty euros. You have to keep a tally. You don't get any money for the first four, so don't write them down; they cover your costs – rent, electricity, etc.'

In fact, the men paid her directly and I didn't handle any money at all. I just waited behind a curtain until she called me into the salon, which was the main room where potential customers looked me up and down and tried to decide if I was worth 20 euros, while the woman described to them with bored indifference all the things I could do.

Some of the men, particularly the young ones, just came to look and had no real intention of 'buying'. Those who did pay their money were given one of three room numbers and directed to the staircase, and I followed them up in a rickety old lift, trying to shut my mind to any thought at all.

It was a single-girl brothel, which meant that I was the only girl working on a particular shift. The woman who ran it was nasty and devious. 'Be quick,' she was always telling me. 'Get your skates on. All three rooms are full. Time is money.' She was obviously running scams, one of which involved removing ten condoms from the table every night, instead of the agreed four, and then insisting that I had made a mistake with my tally. I wasn't in any position to argue with her, and although I was annoyed when I realised what she was doing, it didn't really matter who got the money: whoever it was, it wasn't going to be me.

'You can't touch,' I would say to all the men. Then I would lie on the bed and tell them, as the woman was always telling me, 'Hurry up. Be quick.' Twenty euros bought them five minutes, after which, whether they had finished or not, they had to pay again or go. When I insisted – and I was equally ruthless with all of them – some of them would start kicking off. So I would press the button beside the bed, which alerted the woman down-stairs, who would call one of the Albanian 'bouncers' who always stood outside the house, and he would man-handle the guy out into the street – after beating him up if he was still resisting.

When we were busy, men who decided to pay for extra time would often have to wait while I took the additional 20 euros down to the woman and got rid of the men in the other two rooms. Sometimes they got fed up with waiting and would open the door of the room they were in and start shouting, 'Come on. Where are you?' It took a great deal more to embarrass me than it had done just a few months earlier, but I did feel embarrassed for those men. A lot of the clients were dirty and ill-kempt, and clearly indifferent to what the rest of the world might think about them, while even well-off local businessmen didn't seem to be bothered by the fact that there might be men in the waiting room who would recognise them.

I had more than 50 clients that first night, and by the end of it I was in agony. Elek came to pick me up and dropped me at the hotel, and after I'd had just a few hours' sleep, he took me back to the brothel again. I worked there night after night without a break for several weeks before he moved me on to another place, and after that to another one. Every new brothel was dingy and dirty and almost indistinguishable from the one I had just been working in. The only difference was that in some of them, despite having a consistent average of at least 50 clients every night, I would be told, 'Try something different. You're not doing enough.'

One night, when business was slow, I heard a man tell the brothel owner, 'I've brought my son. He's fifteen and he's a virgin.'

'That's fine,' she said. 'She does virgins. It's forty euros.' I could tell from her voice she was smiling, but I felt sick at the thought that a man would take his son to a place like that.

A few minutes later, when I opened the door of one of the rooms upstairs and found an anxious-looking boy sitting on the edge of the filthy bed, I just wanted to cry. He was the same age as I was, although I felt much older. I tried my best to dissuade him, telling him, 'You're too young. I feel like a paedophile. Please, don't do this. This isn't the way to lose your virginity.' But he was determined, and then angry and humiliated because he couldn't do it.

When I told Elek about it afterwards, how I had hated it and didn't want to do it again, he shrugged and said, 'You have to. It's normal for some Greek men. It's what they do. They bring their sons to brothels to make them into men and to make sure they don't turn gay.' I didn't know much about anything, but even I knew that was ridiculous. After what I had already seen and experienced, however, I suppose I shouldn't have been surprised or disgusted by anything 'some men do'.

When Elek picked me up from the brothels in the early hours of the morning, I would give him half of what I had earned. Then, once a week, he would take me to a Western Union office, where I would send Jak the other half, minus

30 euros, which I was allowed to keep and spend on ciga-rettes and food. One night, Elek couldn't come for some reason, so he told me to walk to the hotel where he would meet me later to collect his money. After he had been and gone, I stayed in the hotel bar and was just finishing drink-ing the coke he'd bought me when the Albanian hotel owner said, 'We've got some girls coming in tonight,' and winked at me as if we shared a secret. I had no idea what he meant, so I just nodded and said, 'Oh, right.' But I was interested enough – and certainly lonely enough – to decide that I would wait to see them.

When eight girls came into the bar a little while later, I didn't recognise the language they were speaking to each other. They were with a Greek man and woman, and as they all sat down, one of the girls smiled at me shyly. Another girl asked the man in English, 'So what is the restaurant like? I haven't worked as a waitress before. Will they teach us how to do it? Doesn't it matter that we can't speak Greek?'

'It's a very nice restaurant,' the man answered. 'And don't worry about the language or about training for the work. You won't have any problems, any of you.'

The girls all nodded and I realised that they must all speak English too. One of them said something in their own language and as they all leaned forward to listen to her, I heard the man say quietly in Greek, 'You don't need much training to be able to lie on your back and open your legs.' And the woman laughed.

I quickly looked away, pretending to cough to cover up the sound of my sharp intake of breath. 'Just stay calm,' I told myself. 'Don't give any sign that you heard what he said.' The blood was pounding in my ears and even when I clutched the edge of the seat very tightly I couldn't stop my body shaking, because I knew what was going to happen to those poor, unsuspecting girls.

I was still struggling to control my rising panic when the Greek couple told the girls they were just going to have a word with the hotel owner – who was now out at the reception desk – and then they walked out of the bar. The girl who had smiled at me when they first came in, and who was sitting at the table nearest to mine, leaned across and said, 'Hello. Do you work here?'

'No,' I answered, forcing myself to return her shy smile. 'I'm … I'm just staying here for a while.'

'We're going to be staying here too,' she said. 'I'm Kasia. I'm from Poland. I go to college there. I've come here to work as a waitress for a while so that I can save some money for my studies. It's the first time I've ever been away from my family. I miss them already, and my boyfriend too. But it's a good job, I think. I can't earn so much money in Poland.'

Apart from a couple of my loneliest clients, it was more than anyone had told me about themselves in months. I suddenly felt desperately sad at the thought that this girl I didn't know was the closest thing to a friend I'd had in all that time. She seemed to be a really sweet girl and I wanted to say something to her, to warn her to get out before it was too late. But I was frightened. Although I didn't know anything about the Greek couple, I knew that the Albanian hotel owner could be violent – I had often seen him hit his wife when he was drunk. Despite my fear, however, I knew that, if there was any chance the girl could escape, I couldn't just turn my back on her and walk away.

I needed to think. So I said something polite to Kasia and went upstairs to my room, where I sat on the balcony smoking a cigarette, trying to clear my head of the white noise of confusion.

Chapter 8

I was still sitting on the balcony when Kasia appeared on the one next door. She seemed pleased to see me there and to have someone to talk to. She told me about her home, her studies in Poland and how she was already feeling homesick. And I explained how I had come to Greece on holiday with my mum and how we had both fallen in love and decided to stay. Then I told her what I had heard the Greek couple say in the bar downstairs.

For a moment she just stared at me, as though her grasp of English had suddenly failed her, and then she burst into tears.

'Hush,' I whispered across the balcony railings. 'Don't let anyone hear you crying. Come round to my room. I'll open the door. But be quiet, for heaven's sake.'

Her face was white and she was shaking when I let her into my room.

'Where are the other girls?' I asked her.

'I don't know,' she said. 'I think they're still downstairs, talking about all the things we're going to do while we're here.' A sob caught in the back of her throat and I put my hand on her arm. 'I'm going to try to help you. It will be all right,' I assured her, although I had no real reason to believe that it would be.

'I've got my phone,' she said, as if she had only just remembered it. 'You can speak Greek. We'll just call the police and ...'

'No, we can't do that,' I interrupted her. 'I don't know if we can trust the police.' Jak had warned me many times that if I ever went to the police, he would know, and I was afraid that even if Kasia didn't mention my name, he would find out somehow that I had been involved.

'What am I going to do?' she wailed. 'I can't stay here. I have to go home. I want my mum and my boyfriend. I came here to work as a waitress. I can't do ... that.'

Suddenly, I remembered the phone number written on the screwed-up piece of paper I had hidden at the bottom of my bag. 'There is *someone* who might help us,' I told Kasia. 'He's a nice guy, and very rich. I'm sure he would buy you a plane ticket home if I tell him what's happened.' In fact, I didn't even know if the bit of paper was still there. But it was, and I had a sense of elation as I smoothed it out and discovered that the numbers written on it were still just legible.

I sent a text to Andreas saying, 'It's Megan. Please phone me urgently on this number.' And my phone rang almost immediately.

'It's lovely to hear from you,' Andreas said, in his quiet, competent-sounding voice. 'I hope this means you're going to come to see me.'

'I need your help,' I told him. 'I'm with a girl who needs to get out of a really bad situation. Will you help us? Please.'

'Come round.' Andreas was instantly serious. 'You know where I am. Get a taxi. I'll pay for it when you get here.'

'I really do think he'll help you to get home,' I said to Kasia. 'First though, we have to get out of here without anyone seeing us.'

I think I was even more scared than she was, because I *knew* what would happen if I got caught trying to help her escape. But I felt proud too, for daring to try to help her when I hadn't ever dared to help myself. Ironically, perhaps, I was so focused on trying to save Kasia, so she wouldn't have to go through what I was going through, that I didn't really think about myself at all. So I didn't consider the possibility that if Andreas could get Kasia out of the country and home, maybe he could do the same for me. In all the scenarios I might have imagined, I was an invisible presence. I suppose that was because in my mind, as well as in the minds of everyone I ever had anything to do with, I was a non-person. The only thing that concerned me at that moment, though, was how to get out of the hotel with Kasia and somehow find my way to Andreas's house.

'Just follow me,' I told the pale, visibly shaking girl. 'Stay close and don't make a sound.' Then I opened the bedroom door very slowly, held my breath and listened for a few seconds, before, very cautiously, putting my head out just far enough to be able to see in both directions along the almost-dark corridor.

I had just stepped out of the room and was turning back to whisper to her to follow me when we heard a loud bellowing shout. Kasia made a whimpering sound and I pulled her out into the corridor, hissing at her, 'Quick! Go into your room and lock the door.' And then I did the same.

It was the hotel owner's voice we had heard; I could tell that he was very drunk and in a rage. Why he was screaming my name and threatening to kill me, I didn't know, nor did I ever find out. Just a few seconds after I had darted back into my room and locked the door, he was hammering on it with his fists. As I stood, flattened against the wall, I could see through the small window above the door the knife he was waving above his head, and I began to pray. Like everything else in the hotel, the door of my room was flimsy and cheaply made, and I knew it wouldn't take him long to bust it off its hinges. There was only one other way out. Shaking and telling myself, 'It'll be all right; just don't look down,' I climbed up on to the worn-stone parapet that surrounded my balcony, took a deep breath and stepped across the three-storey drop to the road below onto Kasia's balcony.

When she saw me appear in front of her, Kasia had to clamp her hand over her mouth to stop herself screaming. My legs were shaking so much I stumbled and nearly fell, and she put her arm round me to help me into her room, where we stood together, listening to the hotel owner ranting and raving and kicking my door. When the noise stopped abruptly, the whole world seemed to fall silent. A few seconds later, I heard the lift door opening and closing, followed by the distinctive whirring sound it made as it moved between floors.

We waited and listened for a minute or two longer, in case it was a trick. Then we crept out into the corridor, ran down the stairs, through the open door of the hotel and out into the street. Luckily, no one saw us and once we were outside we just kept running, following the tramline to the next stop, where we jumped on a tram that would take us to the part of town where Andreas lived. It would probably have made more sense to do what he had suggested and get a taxi. But I was panicking and, fortunately, we didn't encounter a ticket inspector before the tram reached our stop and we jumped off.

When Andreas opened the front door of his expensive townhouse, we almost fell across the threshold. He ushered us into his elegantly furnished living room, and after I had calmed down enough to be able to tell him what had happened, he picked up the phone and booked Kasia a ticket on a flight to Poland.

'Can she stay with you until it's time for her to leave?' I asked Andreas. 'Will you look after her? I have to go back to the hotel.' He promised he would, and I knew he would keep his word.

'And you?' he asked me. 'Are you all right? Don't you want me to book a flight to somewhere for you too?'

'I'm fine,' I lied. 'Just take care of Kasia. You don't have to worry about me.' After all, where would I have gone? Kasia had a mother, a boyfriend and a home in Poland; whereas my mother was living in Greece – not far enough away for me, or her, to be safe from danger – and there was no one waiting for me back in England.

It was fear that was really imprisoning me and preventing me from trying to escape. Elek rarely used violence to control me, as Jak had done. His methods were more subtle – I had seen the gun he kept under the seat of his motorcycle – and I believed him when he told me that someone was always watching me and when he threatened, in the same calm, matter-of-fact voice, that there would be 'massive trouble' if I ever tried to run away.

I didn't want to think about what was going to happen to the other Polish girls. I knew I couldn't help them all. Although the risk I had already taken in leaving the hotel had been worth it for Kasia's sake, I didn't know what would happen when I went back. Any potentially plausible excuse I might be able to come up with – that I had been frightened by the hotel owner, for example – would only be believed if I didn't stay away too long. I had become very paranoid; I was even convinced that my phone was being tracked. So I was also anxious to get away from Andreas's house as quickly as possible in case someone did come after me and found Kaisa there too. The trouble was, the prospect of going back to the hotel was every bit as frightening as not going back. When I think about it now, it seems incredible that I had an opportunity to escape and didn't take it.

Kasia hugged me and thanked me and said she would get in touch as soon as she was safely out of the country. Then Andreas put me in a taxi and I sat on the back seat, praying no one had discovered that both Kasia and I were missing and, if they had, that they wouldn't connect her disappearance with mine.

Andreas had given the taxi driver money and I asked him to drop me off a short distance from the hotel. As I walked quickly along the road with my heart thudding, I kept my head down, hiding my face from anyone who might see and recognise me. Rounding the corner into the road where the hotel was, I heard the sound of voices before I saw the police cars. When I looked up, the hotel seemed to be swarming with police.

My first, excited, thought was that the other girls had somehow found out what was really planned for them and had phoned the police for help. It was only later that I discovered what had actually happened was that when the hotel owner hadn't been able to find me, he had directed his drunken aggression towards his wife. It was someone who had seen him attacking her that had called the police. When they arrived – by the carload – they'd arrested the hotel owner and closed the hotel.

Somehow, Elek had already heard what had happened and my phone started ringing while I was still standing outside, trying to persuade one of the policemen to let me go in.

'Pack up all your stuff,' Elek told me. 'I'll come and get you as soon as I can.'

I didn't know why the hotel owner had been threatening to kill me. At the time I thought it might have been because he had found out I had spoken to Kasia, and therefore he might already have told Elek. So although Elek didn't sound angry when he spoke to me on the phone, I felt sick with anxiety as I waited for him.

Fortunately, the policeman let me go into the hotel to collect my things, and when Elek arrived he was more concerned with other potential problems than with anything I might have been doing before he got there. 'If anyone asks you any questions,' he warned me, 'say you're in Greece on holiday.' By some miracle, I had got away with it. The hotel owner was sent to prison for assaulting his wife and the hotel was shut down. I don't know what happened to the other girls. I hope with all my heart that they went home to their families in Poland.

When he came to pick me up, Elek drove me to another hotel, where he told me to wait until he came back for me. All the places I stayed while I was in Athens were more like doss-houses than hotels; this one was the dirtiest, most cockroach-infested of them all.

The following day, I had a text from Andreas asking if it was okay for him to phone me. After I had texted him back to say that it was, he told me, 'It's good news. Everything went according to plan. Kasia is safely back in Poland. She sent me an email when she got home and she asked me to tell you, "Thank you very much for saving my life." She says she hopes you do well and that she would like to keep in touch with you.'

'Thank you for getting her out, Andreas,' I said. 'I knew you would. I'm really grateful to you.'

Fortunately, as Elek didn't really care what I did as long as he got his money, he rarely checked my phone, so he didn't find out about the call from Andreas. I erased the text messages though, and then I threw myself across the dirty, stained sheet on the bed and cried until I couldn't cry any more. Why hadn't I admitted to Andreas that I wasn't the 'willing' prostitute I pretended to be? Why hadn't I asked him to help me, too? I was glad Kasia had escaped and I was proud of the role I had played in helping her to do so. But I was filled with despair at the realisation that I had missed what might be the only opportunity I would ever have to break the invisible bonds that bound me to a life of unremitting loneliness and humiliation.

When Elek came to pick me up the next day, he took me to a café, where he introduced me to a Greek man, probably in his fifties, called Christoph. After they had spoken to each other briefly, Christoph handed Elek a wad of notes.

'He'll look after you now,' Elek told me. 'I'll see you around.' Then he stood up, shook the other man's hand, and walked away.

I don't know if it's possible to feel any more mortified and ashamed than I did as I sat in the café that day trying to make sense of the fact that I had just been sold. It had happened before, of course, when Leon had bought a 'half-share' in me from Jak, and when he had sold his share on again to Elek. I hadn't understood what was happening then, and I don't think I really even understood it now. As long as I clung to the belief that everything I did was for Jak and me, I could stop my brain trying to process the facts I didn't want to accept. In reality, though, after he had left me in Athens, Jak had never phoned me or answered my calls. He had just sent me a text every few days – no words, just a kiss or a love heart. And then, after a while, I had stopped hearing anything from him at all. The truth I was refusing to face was that his only remaining interest in me was financial.

I'm a stronger person now than I was then, although I still need to work on my confidence and self-esteem. When I look back on that time, I feel angry with myself and incredibly sad. When you truly believe that you're nothing, you don't even consider the possibility that you have a choice about anything. You're like a puppet, waiting for someone to pick up your strings and control your actions. And when the puppeteer puts you down, you don't do anything, because you've got so used to being a puppet you've forgotten that you were ever able to think and act for yourself.

Now that Elek had handed the strings to Christoph, the only thing that changed for me immediately was that it was Christoph who picked me up every morning from the hotel room I shared with a whole army of cockroaches. For the next few months, I continued to work in different brothels around the city, sometimes during the day and sometimes at night. I did some escorting jobs as well, in hotel rooms and in the homes of people who had never even heard the nocturnal sound of an insect's scuttling feet.

I worked alone in some of the brothels; others were studios, where I would be one of two girls working at any particular time and where men would come in, look at us both and then choose between us. For someone with already barely measurable self-confidence, not being picked might have been difficult to process – even when the person doing the picking was just some sleaze-ball who had wandered in off the street. But, by that time, I didn't feel anything at all.

Christoph didn't hit me. In fact, he often praised me. 'Look at you!' he would say. 'You're stunning. You must be proud. You must tell yourself, "I am a good and special person." Go on, say it.' And I was so lonely and so starved of affection that for a moment I *did* feel special, simply because he said I was.

One day he told me, 'You shouldn't be doing this. Why are you doing this?'

'So that my boyfriend and I can build our own house and have a family,' I answered.

'Ah, you will have a lovely place!' Christoph looked into the distance and smiled, as if he, too, could see the image I still clung to. For a while, his words brought definition again to the dream that had begun to fade, and I could almost believe that one day it would become a reality.

Most of the girls who worked in the brothels were Albanian and Romanian, a few were Greek, others were Polish, Russian, Lithuanian and Moldovan. Although I didn't really talk to any of them, I began to suspect that most of them weren't doing the work any more willingly than I was. Even when I worked with other girls in the studios, we rarely spoke to each other. I wanted to talk to them, but when I tried to do so, I think I came across as being needy and a bit weird. The dehumanising effect of what I was doing seemed to have damaged my ability to communicate with other people.

I would see girls out on the streets – students and girls who worked in shops and offices – and I would want to be one of them so badly it was almost like a physical pain. They were living the life I had imagined I would when I came to Athens with Jak. As I watched them laughing and

139

talking to each other, sometimes walking arm in arm, I could feel their energy and confidence, and it would make me sad to realise that I was invisible to them.

When every day is the same and nothing changes, there's no way of keeping track of the passage of time as the weeks become months. So I don't know how long I had been in Athens when Christoph started taking me to different cities to live and work alone in brothels for a few weeks at a time. All the brothels were open for business 22 hours a day, 7 days a week. There were no days off, and it wasn't long before I was completely shattered. They closed for a couple of hours in the early mornings so that the cleaners could come in, and that was when I was supposed to sleep. The problem was that I was usually so far beyond exhaustion, and so hyped up on iced coffee and the energy tablets the brothel owners gave me, that any sleep I did have was restless. Fortunately, there were few customers during siesta time and some of the brothels would close for two or three hours in the afternoons too – and then I would sleep as though I had been knocked unconscious.

The windows of all the brothels were barred and boarded up and I never knew whether it was day or night, which messed up my body clock even more. Apart from the exhaustion, it didn't really make any difference to me though: I wasn't going anywhere, so I had no need to know what time of day or even day of the week it was.

I had, on average, about 50 clients a night. On the worst night of all, 110 men paid to have sex with me. The owner of the brothel I was working in at the time was a man who was quite nice to me, and when I ran out of the back door after my 110th client and was violently sick, he closed up early. I thought that was decent of him – which shows just how distorted my sense of normality had become. But it was certainly more than the owners of most of the other brothels I had worked in would have done.

I was ill after that night – not *because* of it, as it turned out, but because I had a stomach bug. I was already so run down physically that after a few days of severe sickness and diarrhoea, which left me shivering and curled up in agony, I became very weak. Christoph was sympathetic. He called me 'poor girl' and on the days when I was too ill even to get out of bed, he brought me food (which I couldn't eat). He still made me work some nights though, even after I had thrown up on a client, and his apparent concern for me didn't stretch to getting me the hospital treatment I really needed.

After I had been ill for two weeks – by which time I was so painfully thin I looked like one of the walking dead – he moved me to another hotel in central Athens and, at last, took me to a hospital. When the doctor examined me, he said I had Salmonella poisoning and was seriously dehydrated. So they kept me there for a few hours while they put me on a drip. Christoph stayed with me, which I thought was nice of him and a sign that he really did care about me, as he always said he did. It was much later when I realised that what he had actually been doing was making sure I didn't have any direct, one-to-one communication with hospital staff.

As soon as I recovered from the stomach bug, I started doing escort work during the day and working at night in one of the many brothels in the city centre. I would walk back to the hotel at around 6 a.m., sleep till 9, and be ready when Christoph came to pick me up – never later than 10 – to take me to the first of the day's escorting jobs, most of which were in apartments in the nicer areas of the city.

Mum and I texted each other every day and sometimes she phoned me too. I had a special, cheerful voice I used as I described to her how well I was doing in my job as a waitress. It was obviously convincing, because she often said, 'You sound so happy, Megan. I'm so pleased for you.'

'I think Jak and I have split up,' I told her one day, a long time after he had stopped answering even my texts. 'But I've made new friends here and I'm fine about it. In fact, I'm thinking of going to college, to do a beauty course – you know, hair and nails.' I was surprised by how easily the lies came and by the fact that, as I was telling them, I could almost believe I was living the life I was describing.

'I can't wait to see you any longer,' Mum said when she phoned me a few days later. 'You keep putting me off, saying you're busy. And I can understand that you can't spare the time to come here. But what if I came to Athens?

Even if you can't get any time off work, we could at least spend a few hours together.'

'I'll see if I can work something out,' I told her.

It had been a long time since I had last seen her, and although it was what I wanted more than anything else in the world, the thought of her coming to Athens threw me into a state of panic.

Chapter 9

The next time I saw Christoph, I somehow managed to pluck up the courage to say to him, 'My mum wants to come to visit me. You know she lives in Greece now, on the coast? So it's difficult to keep putting her off. And I do *really* want to see her.'

We were in Christoph's car at the time, driving along a busy road on the way to a brothel a short distance from the city. He didn't say anything at all for a minute or two. Then he slowed down, pulled in to the side of the road and stopped the car. When he leaned towards me, I flinched, thinking he was going to hit me. Instead, he opened the glove box, took out a photograph and handed it to me.

Although the image was clear and in focus, it seemed to have been taken through a doorway into a dimly lit room, and I couldn't make any sense of it at first. Then Christoph asked me, pleasantly, 'Is that your mum?' And suddenly I realised that the 'room' was Nikos's bar, and it felt as if someone was shaking my body from the inside.

'Yes,' I whispered, touching the image of my mother with my finger.

'Well, you know what will happen to her if you do anything to make me angry.' Christoph's tone was still pleasant. 'If you ever try to get away ...' He didn't need to finish the sentence. He just looked at me without expression and did the shooting motion he sometimes did, with his fingers pointing at the photograph. Then he smiled, took the photograph out of my hand, put it back in the glove box and said, 'It's a great idea. So, what would you like to do while you're mum's here? We must make sure she has a good time.'

The fact that Christoph had a photograph of my mother seemed simply to be further proof that what he often told me was true and that he had eyes everywhere. The only person who knew where my mum would be was Jak, and I was certain *he* wouldn't have taken the photograph and given it to Christoph. When I saw Jak again, a long time later, he swore he didn't know anything about it, and I believed him. But that was before I realised that almost every emotionally charged, heart-felt word he ever spoke to me was a lie.

'Your mum thinks you're working as a waitress?' Christoph asked me, although it wasn't really a question.

'Right, well that's easy.' He patted my knee and pulled the car back into the traffic. 'We'll plan a nice day in Athens for her.'

'She wants to come for a couple of nights,' I told him, knowing that I was pushing my luck, but that Mum would be hurt – and possibly suspicious – if I insisted on just a one-night visit, particularly when we hadn't seen each other for such a long time. 'It will take her almost a whole day to get here.' I held my breath as I waited for Christoph's reaction. But to my huge relief he just shrugged and said, 'Oh well, I suppose we can manage that.'

He picked me up from the hotel a couple of days later and we went to a café, where he took a photograph of me standing next to the café owner, smiling and holding some cups on a tray. The next day, he gave me a print of the photo and said, 'Put it in your bag. You can show it to your mum when she comes.'

Mum arrived in Athens about a week after Christoph had agreed to her visit. He had booked a room for us in a hotel in the city centre, which turned out to be basic but clean, and in a completely different league from the ones I was used to staying in.

'Tell her you've been given a couple of nights off work,' he had said. 'Eat in a nice restaurant. Enjoy yourself.' He had counted out 250 euros and, as he was putting the notes in my hand, added, 'But don't forget, I'll be watching you, all the time, everywhere you go.'

I was incredibly excited at the thought of seeing my mum again. I had often fantasised about telling her what I was really doing in Athens, and once I knew she was coming, I tried to think of some way of letting her know the truth. Simply blurting it out while she was there wasn't a viable option, because I knew she would insist on doing something, and then both our lives would be in danger. I thought about writing a note and putting it in her pocket so that she would find it when she was at home and safe with Nikos again. But then I imagined her reading it, flying into a panic and phoning me when I was with Christoph, and him realising what I had done, no matter what excuse I tried to make. Or instead of phoning me, she might contact the police, which would be even worse, because I didn't know if we could trust them.

'Focus, Megan,' I kept telling myself. 'There has to be some way of doing this.' But I knew in my heart that there *was* no way out that wouldn't end badly – for me and, if I did anything to involve her while she was in Athens, for my mum too.

When the day finally came, I was so excited I could barely sit still in Christoph's car as he drove me to the coach station. After he dropped me off, I knew he was still there somewhere, watching as Mum stepped down off the coach. We were both crying as we flung our arms around each other. Mum was simply happy to see me, but for me there was an added reason, because it was the first time in more than a year that I had been held by someone who cared about me.

I was aware of Christoph following us on several occasions while my mum was in Athens. At least twice, he drove past in his car and beeped the horn – just to let me know – and I waved and told Mum it was a friend. I'm sure he had other people watching us too. It didn't matter though, because I wasn't going to let anything spoil the few precious hours I had with my mother.

On the first evening, we got a taxi from the hotel to a place by the sea where there are lots of bars and cafés. We bought hotdogs and sat outside a café talking and talking. I kept looking at Mum, trying to memorise everything about her and about the evening we were spending together – an evening I had believed I would never have – and imagining what it would be like to go home on the coach with her.

There was a small amusement park on the seafront, and after we had eaten our hotdogs, we went on some of the rides and I forgot about things for a while and had fun. Then we bought a bottle of wine and went back to the hotel room, where we got a bit drunk and started dancing to music on the radio. A song came on that I knew and I sang along to it in Greek, while Mum sat on the bed and listened. When it had finished, she clapped and told me I was brilliant. 'You've got a lovely voice,' she said. 'And I can't believe how well you speak Greek. I've been so impressed by the way you talk to everyone. I've been here almost as long as you have, and I can barely speak it at all.'

'It's just practice, Mum,' I said. 'If you know people – friends,' I stumbled over the word, 'friends who don't speak

English, you soon learn.' I sounded casual, but in fact I felt incredibly proud of her praise.

It must have been about 2 o'clock in the morning when a man poked his head around the wall that divided our balcony from the one next door and said angrily, 'Hey! Some people are trying to sleep. Keep the noise down.' We *were* behaving badly and the poor man had every right to be fed up with us. But we were drunk, he had a single curl of hair hanging from his otherwise bald scalp, and we couldn't stop laughing.

I hadn't laughed like that, enjoyed myself or had someone to talk to for as long as I could remember, and I didn't want the night to end. We did eventually fall asleep though. When we woke up the next morning we both felt a bit rough, so we sat on the balcony in the sunshine, smoking cigarettes, drinking iced coffee and talking. Mum rang Nikos and then handed the phone to me, saying, 'He wants to talk to you.'

'You must come to see us here very soon,' Nikos said. 'When you next get some time off work, come then. Okay?' And I promised him that I would.

That evening, Mum wanted me to show her where I worked.

'I don't want to go there on my day off,' I told her.

'We won't stay long,' she said. 'I want to be able to imagine you at work. And I want to meet your boss.'

'I'm there all the time. I don't want to take you there today,' I insisted, hating the fact that I sounded like the petulant teenager I sometimes used to be, and that I was lying to her. 'Anyway, I've got a surprise planned for you.'

Mum still moaned a bit, but I knew I'd got myself out of it. And then she suddenly asked, 'Shall I stay another day? I would love to come to the café and have a coffee while you're working. Why don't I do that?'

People say that the most convincing liars are the ones who manage to delude themselves into believing that what they're saying is actually true. I think for me it was simply a case of 'practice makes perfect': I always knew when I was lying to other people – but it was simply something I had to do, every day. I can't remember now how I managed to persuade Mum to stick to her original plan and not stay any longer. What I do remember, though, is that I was really upset because I knew I had hurt her feelings.

What *was* true was that I had planned a surprise for her that night. Using what was left of the 250 euros Christoph had given me, I took her to a port just outside the city to have a meal at one of its fish restaurants. First, we wandered through a marina, trying to decide which of the many massive, incredibly expensive boats we would buy if we had a few million euros to spare. Then I chose a restaurant that had a glass floor and a huge picture window facing the water.

Although it started to rain just as we sat down to eat, we could still see the lights along the coast and watch the illuminated water lapping underneath our feet. As we were still recovering from the excesses of the night before, we decided against drinking any more alcohol with what turned out to be a really good three-course dinner.

At one point, Mum looked at me and said, 'I always wanted the best for you, Megan. I'm *so* proud of you. You're so clever, working and making a life for yourself, and speaking Greek the way you do.' I had to force myself to keep smiling. And as I was desperately searching for something to focus on so that I wouldn't burst into tears and tell her the truth, I remembered the photograph. Taking it out of my bag, I passed it across the table to my mum and said, 'This is the café where I'm working. And this is my boss.'

'Is he good to work for?' She tilted the photograph towards the light. 'Ah, he looks really nice.'

'Yes, he's great,' I said. 'He treats me really well. And the customers are good too. I get loads of tips. That's how I could afford to bring you here this evening.'

'Can I keep this? I want to show it to Nikos, and put it up on the wall in the bar.' When I nodded, Mum put the photograph in her handbag, and I had to look away quickly so that she wouldn't see the tears that escaped before I could stop them. In fact, she scanned the photograph when she got home, and put it on her phone and on Facebook with a note saying, 'This is Megan with her boss at the café where she's working. She's happy and doing really well in Athens.'

The next morning, Christoph texted me to ask what time my mum was leaving and to tell me to wait in the café at the coach station for him when she had gone. Despite what he said, however, I was edgy and anxious as Mum and I said goodbye, because I thought he might already be there, watching.

When Mum walked away from me across the concourse, a little voice in my head was saying, 'Why don't you go with her? Go on, just get on the coach. What's he going to do with all these people around?' I had a sharp pain in my chest and suddenly I couldn't bear the thought of Mum leaving me there on my own. I had just taken a step towards her when she turned, waved to me and mouthed the words, 'I'm so proud of you, Megan.' Suddenly I knew I couldn't tell her the truth, because I *wanted* her to be proud of me, not ashamed. So I forced myself to smile and wave back at her, and then to watch her coach pull out on to the road before disappearing into the traffic.

The only good memories I have of all the years I was in Athens are of those two days I spent with my mother. It still makes me cry when I think about it today

I had been sitting in the café at the coach station for about an hour when Christoph finally turned up. He ordered a coffee for himself and another one for me, asked if my mother had enjoyed her visit, and then said, 'I'm going out of town tonight. You'll be working in a brothel on the coast while I'm away. We'll get your coach ticket when we've had our coffee. Then I'll drop you back at the hotel so that you can pack your suitcase.'

My coach left late in the evening of that day and arrived at the town on the coast in the early hours of the following morning. It was a long and tiring journey, but the worst thing about it was that it gave me time to think – about Mum and about what might have happened if I had gone with her. In reality though, I knew that escaping hadn't ever been an option, because there was nowhere I could go where Christoph wouldn't find me and, one way or another, bring me back into line.

I was met off the coach by a very camp Greek brothel owner called Dimitri, who threw up his hands in horror when he saw me. After making me turn round a couple of times while he examined me, he shrieked, 'Oh my God! We're going to have to get you sorted out right away. First, we need to get you some hair extensions.'

'But I've already got them,' I said.

He lifted a strand of my hair between his thumb and first finger, the way you might pick up a small dead animal by its tail, and said, 'I mean *proper* hair extensions. Then we'll buy you some nice underwear. I don't know what sort of places you've worked in before, but I don't have tramps working for me. My place is five star.'

Four hours and 800 euros later, I had new hair extensions and new nails. It seemed an awful lot of money for Dimitri to have spent, but he would soon recoup his investment.

I hadn't managed to sleep much on the coach and by the time I started work that night, I was really tired. Dimitri's 'five-star' brothel turned out to be every bit as cold, dingy, airless and disgusting as all the other brothels I had worked

153

in. I worked alone, and, despite my make-over, didn't do very well on the first night. In fact, quite a few of the men who came in looked at me and went away again. Some of them obviously had no intention of paying for sex; others presumably found someone they liked the look of at one of the other 50 or more brothels in the area that all competed with each other for customers.

'All the other places seem to be doing better than mine,' Dimitri told me later. 'I'm sick of changing girls. I just need to find the right one and then everything will be okay.'

After two more nights of averaging about 40 customers a night – rather than the 50 or 60 Dimitri was hoping for – it began to look as though I wasn't the right girl either, and my self-esteem sank to an all-time low. It's a very surreal experience, feeling ugly because some disgustingly sleazy guy takes one look at you and decides he would rather have five-minute sex with someone else.

Christoph phoned me every night, and what concerned me far more than feeling ugly was the thought that he would be angry with me when he found out I wasn't doing well. In fact, he was fine about it. 'Just try harder tomorrow,' he said. 'Don't worry about it. You're new there. You'll get busy when people get to know you.' Things never did change, however, and a couple of weeks later I was on a coach again, heading back to Athens.

Christoph met me at the coach station and took me to a hotel in the city centre I hadn't stayed in before. I started doing some escorting during the days, as well as working in brothels at night.

Early one morning, Christoph phoned me and said, 'I'm coming to get you now. Pack your bag and be ready to leave immediately. The police are on my trail.' He sounded stressed, and as soon as I had put the phone down, I started running round the hotel room like a headless chicken, scooping up clothes and things from the bathroom and stuffing them into my suitcase. I didn't have much, so it didn't take me long, and by the time Christoph arrived I was packed and ready to go.

I don't think Christoph had ever been angry with me before that day. But as I sat beside him in the car, he seemed tense and preoccupied and barely spoke to me. It was just a short drive to the apartment building where he parked and told me, tersely, to get out of the car. I had learned a long time ago, as a small child, not to do or say anything that might irritate people who are stressed or in a bad mood. So I followed him silently along the dank, dirty corridor into one of the apartments, where five frightened-looking girls were sitting on the floor in a small, airless room.

'You're going to have to stay here until the police are off our trail,' Christoph told me. He pushed the girl nearest to him with his foot, and she quickly shuffled sideways to make space for me to sit down. The stench in the room was overpowering. The window had been boarded up, but there were slivers of light seeping in around the edges. As my eyes gradually adjusted to the gloom, I could see the faces of some of the girls. Most of them had barely glanced up when we walked into the room.

One of the girls was crying and as she lifted her head to look at me, I saw that her face was swollen and covered with dark bruises. Christoph noticed her too, and suddenly bent down and started punching her. The first time his fist made contact with the girl's cheek, she cried out. Then she just sat there silently, one arm raised in front of her face almost casually, as if she was trying to block the sun from her eyes, and her head jerked violently from one side to the other with every blow.

When Christoph stopped punching her and turned back towards me, I flinched involuntarily. But he didn't hit me. He snatched my bag and threw it across the room so that its contents spilled out over the floor. Then he picked up my passport and phone, put them in his pocket and, bending down again, shouted into my face, 'You've still got a few years' work left in you and you belong to me now. Do you understand?' I nodded my head.

'And you.' He looked round at the other frightened, cowering girls. 'You're nothing more than little whores. Instead of sitting there snivelling, you should be thanking me. You're lucky to have someone like me to protect you. If the police find you, you'll go to prison and then you'll be sent back to where you came from with a criminal record. And don't get any stupid ideas. The neighbours are watching you and I have many friends in the police force. You know what will happen to you if you try to escape.'

It was obvious that the girls understood what he was shouting at them in Greek, so they must have been in the country for at least as long as I had. And they must have felt the same sense of crushing, defeated hopelessness I felt when Christoph turned and walked out of the room, locking the door behind him.

During all the months I had been in Athens, I had learned a lot about fear, including the fact that it comes in many forms – fear of violence, of the unknown, of making a wrong decision when you know your life might depend on it, and when you know there is nothing you can do to help yourself. For a long time after Christoph had left, none of the girls moved or spoke. I didn't dare say anything to any of them because I was convinced that we really were being watched and listened to. And I was afraid because I thought Christoph had lied and that he might never come back for us. Even now when I think about it, I get a tight knot in my stomach.

For a while, I just sat there, staring blindly ahead of me with my mind almost completely blank. Then I began to look more closely at the other girls. Most of them seemed to be about my age or a bit older. But there was one very small girl who was curled up on the floor crying silently and who, I suddenly realised with a sickening sense of shock, was probably no more than eight years old. She seemed to be alone, without her mother, and no one made any move to try to comfort her.

I don't know how long I had been sitting with my back against the wall when I finally plucked up the courage to whisper, 'Is there water? Are we allowed to get a drink?'

'Yeah, there's a tap,' one of the girls answered, without looking at me.

I didn't get up immediately: I waited until my thirst outweighed my fear before tiptoeing across the narrow hallway to the tiny kitchen. I had always drunk bottled water since coming to Greece. Even in Athens, where the tap water is supposed to be safe, I didn't risk drinking it in the sort of hotels I was used to staying in. But by that time I was so thirsty I think I would have drunk whatever had trickled out of the single grimy tap in the kitchen of the apartment.

When I went back into the other room, I asked one of the girls if she knew where the child's mother was. She looked at me for a moment, as if trying to decide whether to answer, and then just shrugged her shoulders. All the other girls were equally unresponsive. Later, when two of them had a brief, whispered conversation, I thought the language they were speaking was Russian. For most of the time, though, we all sat there in silence, thinking our own thoughts, or trying not to think at all.

As the light around the boarded-up window began to fade into darkness, I got up again, took a chipped glass out of the cupboard in the kitchen, filled it with water and took it back into the room, where I gave it to the little girl. Then

I lifted her on to my knees and stroked her dirty, tangled hair until she fell asleep.

There was a narrow, metal-framed bed in one corner of the room, but no one slept on its misshapen mattress. They just lay down on the hard wooden floor, pulled their knees up to their chests like children do, and shut their eyes. I sat with my back against the wall and my arms wrapped tightly around the little girl, and I must have dozed off too, for a while. When I woke up and remembered where I was, I thought for a moment about shouting for help. There were no sounds from the street below to stifle my voice, so someone in one of the other apartments would be bound to hear me, and then they would call the police. But every time I had almost summoned the courage to open my mouth, I heard Christoph's voice in my head saying, 'You know what will happen to you if you try to escape.'

I slept fitfully after that, for maybe a couple of hours, before being woken up by the sound of voices. I was still half-asleep when the two men who had come into the apartment pulled the little girl out of my arms and took her away. I wished at the time that I had been awake enough to have reacted. In reality though, I knew that even if I had been, I wouldn't have been able to do anything to stop them.

I could hear the little girl crying outside the door of the apartment; then the sound became muffled, as if someone had put their hand over her mouth. Still none of the girls said anything and I wondered if, like me, they were trying not to think about where the little girl might be taken. I didn't ever see her again. I often prayed that she hadn't been used for sex and that she was reunited with her mother. At the very least, I hope *someone* looked after her.

Chapter 10

When I was in the kitchen earlier in the night getting water, I had seen a loaf of bread on the work surface. It was hard and stale and splattered with blue patches of mould. But there was nothing else to eat and at intervals throughout the rest of the following day we went into the kitchen one by one and picked bits off it. It didn't make any difference to how hungry I was, but at least it gave me a reason to stand up and move around.

It was starting to get dark on the second night when the door of the apartment opened again. This time, it was Christoph who came in, followed by a short, heavily built man wearing a crumpled shirt and oily jeans. No one said anything; the man just looked at us and then he pointed at me.

'Right, get up,' Christoph said. 'This is a job for you.' Even when he nodded towards the narrow bed in the corner, I didn't understand what he meant. Then the man began to unzip his jeans and it finally dawned on me that Christoph expected me to have sex with him right there, in the room where all the other girls were sitting.

Bizarrely, one of the first thoughts that came to me was that I hadn't had a shower for two days. It wasn't something I needed to worry about on the man's behalf, however. I think I could have been caked in mud from a pigpen before he'd have noticed, or cared, as he climbed on top of me, had sex with me – without using a condom – and then zipped up his jeans and followed Christoph out of the apartment.

I had long ago lost count of the disgusting things I had done – and that had been done to me – since I had been in Athens. Many of them were things I hadn't previously known anyone did, and that I wouldn't have believed I would ever do. By comparison with some of them, having sex with a man in a room full of people was relatively mundane, but it still made me feel physically sick.

Christoph came back again that evening, this time with a different man who chose a different girl. And then no one came at all.

I had been in the room for four days, without any food and surviving only on water from the tap, by the time Christoph did come back. In just those four days I seemed to have gone from thin to emaciated, so that the dirty, creased skirt I was wearing was falling off me, and there was a persistent throbbing pain in my head that felt as if someone was beating the inside of it with a hammer.

According to the clock in Christoph's car, it was mid-morning when he drove me to a hotel, where he told me to have a shower, get dressed and do my make-up. 'Make yourself look really nice,' he said, in his old friendly voice. 'I've got an important job for you.' All I wanted to do was fall on the bed and sleep. But there were no choices in the world I was living in. Perhaps that's why I sometimes react badly today when people tell me what to do: after all those years of being controlled, the anger builds up inside me like steam in a pressure cooker and if I don't release it from time to time, I'm afraid it might explode.

I didn't ever feel angry then, though. I was too exhausted – both mentally and physically – to summon up the energy that would have been required. So while Christoph sat in my hotel room, chatting in the way he used to do in the days before I had seen him punch a girl repeatedly in the face, I had a shower, got dressed and made myself look, if not nice, at least presentable.

When I was ready, he took me to a fast-food restaurant and ordered chicken souvlaki, saying, 'It's what you like, isn't it?' But despite having had nothing to eat for four days, I barely managed more than a few mouthfuls. Then Christoph drove me to one of the wealthiest suburbs of the city, where he said I was going to see a 'very special client'.

163

While we were in the car, he told me what had happened to precipitate the need to 'lie low' for a few days. Apparently, a girl had escaped and gone to the police. 'People are already on the way to Albania to sort out her family,' Christoph said. 'She's a dead woman.' He held out two fingers and mimed the firing of a gun. And although I tried to look as though I was shocked by the unknown girl's treacherous behaviour, what I was actually thinking was that I was *never* going to get away from the unbearable life I had become trapped in.

Christoph stopped the car outside a smart hotel and phoned the client to say we had arrived. Then he told me the room number and said he would be back for me in an hour. It was the sort of hotel where, even if I hadn't been scrawny and had dark rings under my eyes, my cheap clothes would make me look very obviously out of place. So my heart was racing as I walked through the lobby towards the lift, and I was amazed, as well as relieved, when no one stopped me; the receptionist barely even seemed to notice me.

When I knocked on the door of the hotel room, it was opened almost immediately by a pleasant-looking man, who greeted me politely. For some reason, he made me feel safe and I remember hoping that he might decide to book me for longer than the hour, so that I could postpone the moment when I had to go back out into the real world again.

I always showered before and after every client. In good hotels like this one, it was a pleasure to stand under the powerful jet of warm water for a few minutes before wrapping myself in a soft, freshly laundered towel. When I walked out into the bedroom, the man smiled and said, 'Come here.' Then he gently unhooked the towel and let it drop on to the floor.

'You're one of the best he's ever sent,' he told me, smiling again as he looked me up and down. 'It's okay. You can put the towel back on now.' He reached into the breast pocket of his jacket, pulled out his wallet and handed me some money. I had just turned away from him to put the notes in my bag when he said, 'You're under arrest.'

It took a moment for his words to sink in, and then I started to cry. 'Please don't hurt me,' I begged him. 'Here, take the money back.' I tried to push the notes into his hand.

'It's too late,' he said. 'You've already taken it. Put it in your bag and get dressed.'

After I had pulled on my skirt and top, I asked him, tearfully, 'What's going to happen to me?'

'Listen to me,' the man said, grasping my arm and pushing me out of the room ahead of him. 'Just tell the truth and you'll be okay. We're not interested in you. All we want from you is to tell us about the man who brought you here. Do you understand?' I nodded miserably. 'So, are you going to tell the truth?'

'Yes. Yes, of course,' I said.

'Well, in that case, you'll be fine.'

I still didn't understand what had happened. Christoph had spoken to this man on the phone from the car. Did that mean that Christoph had set me up? It didn't make any sense, particularly if what the policeman had just said about not being interested in me was true. But if Christoph *hadn't* set me up and I said something to the police that enabled them to get to him through me … I heard his voice in my head saying, 'People are already on the way to Albania to sort out her family. She's a dead woman.' And suddenly, although I was very afraid of what the police might do to me, I knew I had far more reason to be afraid of Christoph.

On the way out of the hotel, the policeman nodded to the receptionist as if to say thank you, and I realised why she had only glanced at me when I came in and then looked away again without questioning me. It hadn't been because I didn't stick out like a sore thumb among all the well-dressed hotel guests; it was because she had known what I was and what was about to happen to me. Despite the very serious trouble I was in and the fact that I was being led, handcuffed, through the lobby of an expensive hotel, it was that thought as much as any other that made me blush with embarrassment and humiliation.

As we were walking out through the main entrance of the hotel, I heard what I thought was the sound of a car backfiring and then people shouting. I froze and pulled back from the doorway and the policeman tightened his grip on my arm. The street outside the hotel seemed to be full of police. Christoph's car was still parked where it had been when I left him, but now all its doors were wide open.

And then I saw Christoph, shouting and spitting at the three policemen who were half-dragging him down the road back towards the hotel. Stepping out of the hotel into the scene that was unfolding outside seemed unreal, like walking on to a film set or watching yourself in a dream.

Apparently, it had taken several men – including some construction workers on a building site next to the hotel – to catch Christoph when he jumped out of his car and tried to escape. Shots had been fired and it took three policemen to manhandle him, struggling and swearing, into a police car. I was put into another car parked next to the one he was in, and when I looked up, he shook his head, winked at me and mouthed, 'Everything will be fine.' But I didn't see how that could possibly be true.

The police station they took us to, separately, was about a ten-minute drive from the hotel. They left us in a waiting room there, sitting side by side for about an hour, while they went off to do whatever it was they had to do. The police officer at a desk on the other side of the room didn't seem to be interested in anything we might say to each other.

'Are you okay?' Christoph asked me.

When I lied and told him that I was, he held my gaze and said, more loudly, 'I don't understand what's going on. What have you done? Why have the police arrested you? I'm sorry if you're in some kind of trouble. But I don't know you. All I did was give you a lift to the hotel because my friend asked me to do it.'

167

I made a small movement with my head to show him I had understood what he was telling me: that he expected me to take the rap and to say that we didn't know each other. He seemed quite relaxed, almost as if he was enjoying playing the role of injured innocent. If he *was* concerned about what I might say to the police, he didn't show any signs of it. And he didn't need to worry: I had got the message and I would do what I was told, whatever the consequences might be for me.

After we had been at the police station for about half an hour, Christoph's wife arrived with an oxygen cylinder and a face mask. I didn't understand most of the explanation she gave the police officer. Whatever it was, she must have been convincing, because he let her give the cylinder and mask to Christoph. Perhaps Christoph really did have some sort of heart or lung condition. Or maybe it was an elaborate excuse to give his wife access to him in the police station. Whatever the truth of it was, she kept glaring at me in a way that suggested she would quite happily have cut off *my* oxygen supply given half the chance. After she'd gone, Christoph and I were led away to separate cells.

There were 12 women in the cell I was taken to. I could feel the eyes of every one of them looking me up and down as the policeman unlocked the metal-barred gate. I was so frightened and so completely out of my depth it felt like I imagine an out-of-body experience must feel. However, most of the women were friendly and happy to talk to me. It was ironic that, having longed for someone to talk to, I had finally got my wish in the cell of a police station.

Some of the women were prostitutes, and when one of them asked me why I had been arrested, I told her, very briefly, what had happened. 'Whatever you do,' she said, her voice low and earnest, 'don't *ever* say anything. Don't tell the police what you've just told me. Believe me, I know this business. The only way to survive is to keep your mouth shut.' And I knew that she was right.

Because I was used to Christoph talking to me in a friendly way, I think I had been lulled into believing that he really was fond of me – as he often claimed to be. But after what he had said about the Albanian girl who had run away, and after I had seen him assault the girl in the apartment, my illusions about him had been shaken, if not shattered completely. I knew he would protect himself ruthlessly and that if he got into trouble with the police because of something I said, he would turn on me in exactly the same way he had turned on the other girls. What I was also beginning to understand was that in order to save Christoph's skin – and ultimately to protect myself from him – I was going to have to take full responsibility for working illegally as an underage prostitute. I didn't know what that would entail or what the outcome of it all would be, but I was very frightened by the prospect of what lay ahead.

There was a small, barred window high up on one of the walls of the cell, and by the time the light from it had gone,

169

some of the girls were already asleep on the thin, hard mattresses that were strewn across the floor. Although I was exhausted, I knew I wouldn't be able to sleep. So I was still sitting on the wooden bench at the side of the room when two young Albanian girls – certainly no older than me – were brought into the cell, crying.

I spoke to one of them in Albanian and she asked me, 'Who is Christoph? Why are the police asking us about someone called Christoph?' All the threats and warnings I had been given – by Jak, then Leon, Elek and finally Christoph – had made me paranoid, and my first thought was that it might be a trick. What if the two girls had been brought in – by the police or even by Christoph himself – for the sole purpose of seeing if I would say anything? So I shrugged and said I didn't know anyone called Christoph.

It was only when a policeman came into the cell a little while later and started questioning the two girls that I realised they were genuine, and I began to piece together some of their story. Apparently, the Albanian girl whose escape had resulted in me, five other girls and a child being locked in the apartment for four days – and whose own days, according to Christoph, were now numbered – had gone to the police and told them all about him. It was when they found his number on her phone that they had called him and set up the meeting at the hotel.

When they had arrested Christoph, they had seized all the phones they'd found in his car. On one of them there had been texts about two Albanian girls who were arriving that day at the railway station in Athens, and who had consequently been met by police officers. I genuinely don't think the two girls had any idea what was going on. When they left Albania, they had probably been really excited at the prospect of earning good money working as waitresses in Athens. Instead, they were about to spend the night on the floor of a cell in a police station in a foreign country.

I really hoped it would all get sorted out for them and that the police would realise they weren't to blame in any way. In fact, they were incredibly lucky. I don't suppose they could even have imagined what would have happened to them if Christoph hadn't been arrested on that particular day, and if it had been him rather than two police officers who had met them at the railway station. A night on the floor of a cell was a very small price to pay for having escaped the fate they came so close to sharing with me.

From time to time during the night, one of the policemen would ask if we wanted something to eat or drink. I had reached that stage when you're too hungry to eat, but I did have some water. Then I lay down on one of the mats on the floor, covered myself with a threadbare blanket and tried to sleep. I must have dozed off for a while, and when I woke up I talked to another Albanian girl, called Flori, who was waiting to be deported and was having to leave her two children in Greece with her husband's family. Every time she talked about the children, she cried. I felt incredibly sorry for her and I was reminded, once again, that however bad things seem, there's always someone worse off than you are.

Flori and I were sitting talking quietly to each other – I think we were the only ones still awake by that time – when one of the policemen unlocked the gate and came into the cell. For a while, he and his colleague, who stayed outside, chatted and laughed with us. Then the policeman who had come into the cell said, 'You're very sexy. Why don't you do a pose for us?'

I had been very frightened when I was arrested and I was still scared, because I didn't know what was going to happen the next day or the day after that. But I had felt safe in the police station and I was shocked and unnerved when I realised he wasn't joking.

Flori said 'No!' at the same time as I did. And suddenly the policeman's attitude changed completely. 'Get up! Now!' he shouted at us. 'Put your hands on the wall and spread your legs.' I could hear the other women grumbling as they woke up and when one of them said something, the policeman spun round and shouted at her too.

My heart was racing as I stood with the palms of my hands pressed against the damp stone wall. And then, while one of the men touched our bodies, his colleague took photos on his phone and they both laughed and said lewd, disgusting things to us.

The other women must have seen it all before, and most of them pulled the dirty blankets over their heads and went back to sleep. For me though, it was another tremor in the small amount of solid ground that remained under my feet, another naïve illusion shattered. I had been stupid to believe that anywhere was safe for someone like me, a prostitute who didn't matter. I did what I always did at times like that: I thought about my mum and wished I was at home with her, and then thanked God that she couldn't see me now.

The next morning, I was handcuffed and driven to court in a police car, accompanied by three police officers, who were nice to me and said that everything would be all right as long as I told the truth.

I kept asking myself how it had all happened. How had a mildly disaffected schoolgirl who was trying to get her mother's attention by bunking off school become a prostitute and end up sitting in the back of a police car on her way to court in Athens? I knew I had sometimes been wilful and difficult, but had I really been bad enough to deserve the miserable life I was now leading? I didn't think so. But I knew I must be wrong and that what had happened to me must somehow be my fault.

When I walked into the waiting room at the court house, Christoph was already there. He looked up as I came in with the three policemen and nodded almost imperceptibly. Then he turned and said something to the man in the well-cut suit sitting next to him.

One of the policemen took off my handcuffs and said, 'We just have to wait now. We don't know how long it will be before your case is called. When it is, we'll come in with you. And he'll be there, too.' He indicated Christoph with a movement of his head before adding, scornfully, 'And his lawyer.'

When our case was finally called and I was waiting to go into the courtroom, Christoph stood behind me and said, very quietly, 'Whatever they say, they can't prove you know me. Just tell them I gave you a lift to the hotel as a favour to a man you know but whose name you can't remember. Tell them you've never met the man who gives you the work; you've only ever spoken to him on the phone.'

We stood side by side in the courtroom: the three policemen, me, Christoph, his lawyer and the two frightened, bemused Albanian girls who had been within a hair's breadth of becoming prostitutes. We had to say our names and then the judge asked me a question in Greek. I didn't quite catch what she said, partly because Christoph's lawyer started saying something while she was still talking. The judge told him, sharply, to shut up. Then she looked at me again and said, 'Yes or no? It's a simple question.'

'Yes,' I said.

Suddenly everyone in the courtroom was looking at me. When I glanced anxiously at Christoph, he seemed to be on the verge of panic, and his lawyer was glaring at me furiously.

'Clear the court,' the judge ordered. I had begun to shuffle out with the others when she pointed her finger at me and said, 'No, not you. You stay.' As Christoph reached the doorway, I saw him turn his head and look at me with an angry, threatening expression that sent a chill through my body.

As soon as the courtroom had been cleared, I told the judge, 'I don't think I really understood the question. Can you speak in English?' She must have thought I was stupid and that I would have a very limited grasp of my own language too, because she spoke very slowly, saying, 'I asked you if you had been trafficked, and you answered "Yes."'

'Oh no! No, that's not true,' I said, wiping the sweat from my hands on to my crumpled skirt. 'No, no. I'm really sorry. I can't believe I said that.'

She looked at me coldly for a moment. Then she made an irritable clicking noise with her tongue, sighed and told the court officer to let everyone back into the courtroom. I forced myself to look directly at Christoph as he walked in, and I prayed that somehow he would be able to tell from the expression in my eyes that I was sorry.

After the judge had explained to everyone that I had made a mistake, I related the story of how I had ended up in a car with a man I didn't know. Then she asked Christoph why the police had found thousands of condoms in the boot of his car, 10,000 euros and the passports of numerous women in the glove box, and a small arsenal of weapons under the driver's seat.

'I can't answer this question,' Christoph told her, his self-confidence clearly restored, 'because it is not my car. It is a car I borrowed from a friend, who I haven't seen or heard from in a long time.'

'And what is this friend's name?' You could tell by the way the judge asked the question that she already knew that the name he would give her would belong to a man who didn't exist.

A few minutes later, the hearing was adjourned and Christoph and I were driven back, separately, to the police station.

I saw Christoph briefly when we got back to the police station. We passed each other in the corridor and he gave me a warning look. Then I was taken into a small office where four police officers started firing questions at me. They were really pushing me to give them answers, I suppose in the hope that I would eventually slip up and tell them what they wanted to know.

'You know him, don't you?' one of the policemen asked. 'Why don't you tell us the truth? You know him and he's *making* you work. He's trafficking you, isn't he? Answer the question.'

'I don't know him,' I insisted. 'He just gave me a lift.'

'Well, if you're working for yourself, you must have some money. How much are you earning? How much have you got saved? What do spend your money on?'

'I spend everything I earn,' I said. 'I buy clothes. I go out. That's why I haven't got any money saved up. I like the work I'm doing. I just want you to leave me alone.'

I felt almost pleased with myself for outwitting the policemen and protecting Christoph, even though, by lying to them and refusing to answer their questions, I was blocking any attempts they might have made to help me. But I knew I couldn't trust anyone, particularly after the way the two policemen had treated me and Flori in the cell the previous night.

In fact, I thought it was all part of an elaborate test. Christoph had told me many times that he had contacts in the police, and I was (almost) certain that if I did say anything, they would tell him and he would send people to kill my mum, and then me. I was sure that the advice the girl had given me the night before was right and that the only way to survive was to keep my mouth shut. So I stuck to my story and answered their questions without telling them anything.

Despite the fact that they were firing questions at me, I think, to begin with, the policemen wanted me to believe that they were on my side. Eventually, though, as their patience began to wear thin, they started getting really annoyed with me and one of them suddenly pushed back his chair, stood up and said, 'Come with me. Come.'

As I walked out of the room and into the corridor behind him, I heard a sharp sound like something cracking, and when he opened another door, I saw Christoph. He was slumped on a chair and a man was slapping him repeatedly across the face. I gasped and the man stood upright, stretching the muscles in his back. Then Christoph turned his head and looked at me, and I felt a surge of sympathetic affection for the weak, wounded old man he appeared to be. That sounds absurd, I know, that I felt sorry for the man who sold me many times every day to anyone who was willing to pay a few euros to have sex with me. Unlikely as it may sound, though, it is possible, when no one cares about you at all, to become attached to the one person who sometimes says nice things to you.

I felt guilty, too, because I thought that what was being done to Christoph was *my* fault. 'Please don't let them hit him,' I said to the police officer who had opened the door. 'He's done nothing wrong. You have to believe me. I barely even know him. He was just helping out a friend by giving me a lift.'

The policeman didn't answer. He just closed the door and opened another one, a little further along the corridor. One of his colleagues followed us into the small, cramped office and suddenly I felt really frightened because I was certain that the moment had come when, somehow, they were going to force me to tell them the truth.

Instead of doing any of the things they do in films, though, one of the policemen took a bottle out of a cupboard, put a glass down on the table in front of me, poured whisky into it and said, 'Drink that. It'll help you to calm down.'

Seeing Christoph looking tired and almost defeated, when I was used to him being strong and totally in control, had really upset and unnerved me, and I was crying. In fact, I cried a lot of the time when I was in the police station. So although I hated the taste of alcohol, I only hesitated for a moment before lifting the glass to my lips and taking a sip of the whisky.

'Drink more,' the policeman shouted, snatching up the glass and gripping my chin in his strong fingers as he tried to force it into my mouth. 'Drink it. You *will* speak to us. We need to know the truth.' Then he thrust the glass into my hand and as soon as I had drunk the whisky he filled it up again.

'We need you to tell us the truth,' the other policeman said, sternly but more calmly. 'We've been after this man for a long time. We *have* to stop him. Isn't that what you want too? All we need is one person to tell us the truth so that we can nail him. And then it will all be over.'

I don't know if it was the whisky that turned my fear into panic, or if it was guilt because I had been struggling with the thought that time might be running out for the girls in the apartment. But suddenly I burst into tears. 'There are other girls,' I said, the words tumbling out of my mouth as though they were trying to escape before I changed my mind. 'There are other girls who need help. I've seen them. They're locked in an apartment. There was a child there too – she was just a little girl. But men came and took her away. Please, you have to help them.'

One of the policemen put his hand on my shoulder and I saw him exchange a look of quiet triumph with his colleague, which faded instantly when I added, in a completely different, sly tone, 'But I don't know *him*. I don't know who he is.'

It was almost as if someone was flicking a switch in my head that was making my emotions veer wildly between guilt and fear – for myself, for all the other girls who were trapped in the same spiral of hopeless despair and, paradoxically, for Christoph. I was desperate to get away from him: whatever some people prefer to believe, no one in their right mind would ever willingly live the sort of life I was living. The only way I had been able to survive at all was by locking my emotions in a box and throwing away the key. But I was scared, not only *of* Christoph, but also because I had been so brainwashed by him and by the controlling men who had owned my life before him that I didn't know what would happen to me if I was set free.

One thing I did realise, however, was that I was damned if I did tell the truth and damned if I didn't. If Christoph went to prison because of something I said, he would send one of his people after me and, even more importantly, after my mother. If I didn't say anything to the police, I would be condemning to a life of misery and abuse all the other girls he had already trafficked and all the ones he would go on to trick in the future. It felt like a huge responsibility and an impossible choice. What swayed it for me in the end, though, was the thought of something terrible happening to my mum.

The two policemen continued to fire questions at me for what seemed like hours. And I continued to stick to my story, until eventually I was taken back to the cell.

The next day, I was released, and as I walked out of the police station with Christoph, he handed me 50 euros and said, 'Good girl. Go back to the hotel. I'll be in touch.'

Chapter 11

I took a taxi back to the hotel, where I had a shower and then sat on the bed, not knowing what to do or what was going to happen next. I didn't have to wait long. Christoph called that evening to say everything was back to normal and he was coming to pick me up.

As he was driving me to a brothel that night, he told me again that I was a 'good girl'. 'You're one of the clever ones,' he said. 'You're not like the other girls. You're special. I can trust you. I love you, you know.' Only a fool would have believed him. Or someone who was so starved of affection and convinced of her own worthlessness that she clutched with both hands at the pathetic straw of comfort that was being offered to her.

I don't know what happened with the police. Christoph told me some time later that the court hearing had been adjourned, and then I never heard anything more about it. I didn't do any more daytime escorting for a while after that. Instead, I worked in one of four different brothels every night, and occasionally during the day as well. None of them was far from the hotel I was staying in, so I would often walk to them on my own and then back again the next morning. Christoph ordered takeaways for me and phoned me regularly, and when I wasn't working or sleeping, I sat in my dingy hotel room texting my mum.

Despite the fact that everything got back to normal pretty quickly – or, at least, to what I had learned to accept as normal – it wasn't long before something seemed to have changed.

'What's up with you?' Christoph asked me. 'You used to make at least three thousand euros a day and now you're not earning anything like that.'

'Maybe people just don't have the money to spare,' I said. 'I *am* trying my best.'

'Look at you!' He put his hand under my chin and jerked my head upwards. 'You've got bags under your eyes. Don't you get enough sleep? How many times have I told you that when you're not working you should be sleeping, not messing about? You can have showers when you wake up, or at work when things are quiet. Come on, Megan. You have to do better than this.'

It wasn't long after that when he took me to a small town several miles outside Athens, where he left me to work in a brothel that was one of maybe ten on the same road. He came back a couple of times every week to collect the money I had earned. Sometimes the woman who ran the brothel would say, 'You and I will keep the money for the next customer who comes in and not tell Christoph.' But although she was nice to me, I couldn't be sure she wasn't setting me up. So I always said, 'I can't. I have to be loyal to him.' What good would the money have been to me anyway?

One day, the woman told me, 'I've just had a phone call from Christoph. From now on, when I introduce you in the waiting room, I'm to say that you do a "no-condom programme" for twenty euros more.'

I didn't know much about AIDS, and even less about other sexually transmitted diseases; but I knew enough to be horrified by the prospect of having unprotected sex with the sort of men who visited the brothel. I had occasionally had to do it before then, but not as part of a regular 'programme' – for an extra 20 euros that wasn't going to be of any benefit to me.

Although he did sometimes hit me, Christoph wasn't as violent as Jak had been. So it wasn't really because I was afraid of him that I didn't ask him not to make me do it. I had been in Athens for more than four years by that time, and I was so used to doing whatever I was told to do that I simply accepted the fact that I had no choice – about who I had sex with and under what conditions, or about anything else. I was very anxious though, which, as it turned out, I was right to be.

I had been living and working at the brothel for a few weeks when Christoph arrived at 2 o'clock one morning to drive me back to Athens. I must have fallen asleep after just a few minutes, so I don't know how long he had been driving when I woke up to find that he had stopped the car at the side of the road and opened his trousers. When I had done what he told me to do, he started kissing me, telling me how special I was and that he loved me.

I hadn't seen or heard anything from Jak for months. I had already been vulnerable when I met him, and I was far more emotionally fragile and defenceless by the time Christoph told me he cared about me. It was true that he was significantly older than my own father and that he was selling me as a prostitute many times every day. But I was lonely and starved of affection, and wanted to believe that *someone* cared about me.

At some point during every day after that, Christoph had sex with me. He always did it without a condom and he would often slap me and pull my hair so hard it felt as though my scalp was on fire and my neck was going to break. Sometimes he would say afterwards, 'That was shit. You made it really boring for me. What's your problem? Don't you like me?' The sad fact was that I *did* like him; that's what's so difficult to understand when I think about it now. I just didn't like having sex with him any more than I had liked having it with Jak.

The stomach cramps I used to get whenever I had my period had more or less stopped. So I couldn't understand why, after I had been back in Athens for a few weeks, I started getting stomach pains that were far worse than any I had ever had before. By the time I realised they weren't cyclical and I was getting them almost every day, I had developed a burning sensation too, as though my kidneys were on fire. Eventually, the pain got so bad that I had to stop whatever I was doing when it started, so that I could curl into a ball and clutch my knees to my chest.

It happened one night when Christoph was driving me to work. I suddenly felt sick and my whole body seemed to be covered in goose bumps. When I told him about the pain, he reached across and hit me in the face with such force I almost bit right through my tongue. I was so shocked by what he had done that when he gripped my chin and turned my head so that I was facing him, I blinked and then cringed in anticipation of his next blow. Instead of hitting me again, however, he looked at me for a few seconds and then said, 'We'll go to the doctor in the morning and get you checked out.'

I still had to work that night, regardless of the pain. The woman at the brothel gave me painkillers, which didn't really help much. In fact, I don't know how I managed to have sex at all; a lot of the men who visited the brothels were rough, but they seemed to be worse than ever that night. Somehow, I did get through it, and the next day Christoph took me to the doctor.

When Christoph picked me up in the morning, he said, 'You need a blood test, a urine test and a gynaecological examination.' I only had the standard health certificate required by all visitors to Greece, and I assumed that he wanted me to have the tests so that I could get the papers I needed to work in a brothel. But at 18, I was still three years below the age at which it's legal to work as a prostitute in Greece.

After I'd had all the tests done, he drove me to another town where I was going to be working in yet another brothel. We picked up the owner of the brothel en route – a tough-looking, heavily pregnant woman called Kyra, who more or less ignored me but chatted with Christoph as though the two of them were old friends. When Christoph stopped the car outside the brothel – which was a house on a main road that ran through the centre of the town – Kyra got out, hitched up her dress and urinated on the pavement in full view of everyone driving past. That's when I first began to suspect that her establishment might not even be as 'five star' as Dimitri's had been.

After Kyra had shown me round, she and Christoph went with me to the apartment I would be staying in. Then Christoph left, and for the next few weeks Kyra picked me up every morning or evening, depending on what shift I was doing, and drove me to the brothel, where for the next 15 hours I had between 80 and 90 customers. In most other respects, it was much the same as all the other places I had worked: the building was dismal and run-down, and the men were almost indistinguishable from each other. Kyra was pretty much like every other brothel keeper I had come across, except perhaps for being a bit more cocky and the fact that she was a borderline certifiable psychopath. But there was one fundamental, incredibly important difference between working at Kyra's brothel and at any of the others: when I finished work and went back to the apartment, I could go out.

It was a very weird but really good feeling just walking around on my own. Even after a 15-hour shift when I was exhausted, I wanted to do it even more than I wanted to sleep. Sometimes I would go out during the day, sometimes at night, depending on what shifts I was doing. I often went to a café not far from the apartment, which was beside a stream and a lovely stone bridge. I couldn't buy anything, because I didn't have any money, but I didn't care. I was happy just sitting there, drinking a glass of water and watching people.

I would try to imagine that I was one of the other people sitting in the café or walking along the path beside the stream, someone living a normal life, with a job, a home, a family and friends. It wasn't easy, not least because I had no idea what it would be like to be one of those people. I felt detached from everyone else, as though there was some invisible barrier between them and me that kept me apart and separate. It didn't really matter though: just being able to watch them was enough.

You would have thought that being able to wander around in the real world might have made me think about running away. Odd as it may sound, I didn't even consider it. If you've ever had the sort of migraine that whites out your peripheral vision, you might be able to understand what it was like: the only thing I could see was what was directly ahead of me, which was my life as a prostitute; everything else was blurred and out of focus. Even if Christoph hadn't had my passport, I think I would still have been too afraid and too distrustful – of the police and everyone else – to have gone to anyone for help. I don't know if Christoph was aware that I went out. He had certainly made sure – as Jak, Leon and Elek had done before him – that when he wasn't there to control me, the paranoia he had encouraged in me would do the job instead.

After I had been working at the brothel for a few days, Kyra took me to a local hospital to get the results of the tests I'd had done in Athens. I wouldn't have known most of the medical terms the doctor used if he had said them in English, and I certainly didn't understand them in Greek. What I did understand, though, was that there was a problem and that I was going to have to return to the hospital for treatment.

Kyra told the doctor she would explain it all to me properly later. But when we got outside, she just handed me the piece of paper he had given her, jabbed at it angrily with her finger and made a disgusted sort of 'pfffing' sound. She kept repeating a word and telling me I was dirty, until I finally realised that what she was saying was that I had syphilis. The only thing I knew about syphilis was that it was what killed Henry VIII (although I don't think people believe that anymore); I thought it was incurable and that I was going to die.

'You're a dirty tramp.' Kyra spat the words at me. 'Well, you can't work for me anymore. I only have clean girls working in my brothel.' It was ridiculous to accuse me of being dirty: it wasn't *my* choice to be having unprotected sex with hundreds of 'dirty' men; it was something she and Christoph were making me do. I didn't see it like that at the time though. I thought she was right and that it was my fault, and I felt humiliated, contaminated and unclean.

Christoph picked me up later that night and drove me back to Athens. It was a long journey and he stopped periodically, sometimes to buy bottles of beer for me and sometimes so that I could do things to him. Although I still hated the taste of alcohol, I had begun to appreciate the false sense of cheerful confidence it gave me and I drank it whenever I got the chance. That night, I drank the bottles of beer Christoph bought for me as if they were water. So I was a bit drunk by the time we got back to Athens and Christoph dropped me off at the hotel, which was the one I had been staying in before I went to work at Kyra's brothel. Fortunately, I was so tired I fell asleep before the effects of the alcohol wore off, and I was able to postpone the moment when I would have to face the miserable reality of my situation.

I had second-stage syphilis, which apparently meant I must have had it for about a year. Christoph came with me to the hospital and took the same course of tablets that I was prescribed – because he would already have caught it from me, he said. I suppose that's why he still had sex with me afterwards, although less frequently than he had done before and always using a condom. I felt really bad about what had happened, and I thought Christoph didn't love me anymore because of it – which, when I think about it now, isn't as incongruous as the fact that I believed he had ever loved me at all.

Sometimes when he came to pick me up to take me to a job, his wife would be in the car. When she had come to the police station that day, with the oxygen tank I had never seen Christoph use before or since, she had looked as though she was only just managing not to spit in my face. Her feelings towards me didn't change, and I always felt very uncomfortable when she was there. And now, of course, I had an added reason for being embarrassed, because I was having sex with her husband. Ironically, and completely unfairly, Christoph blamed me for the fact that he couldn't have sex with his wife because I had given him syphilis! He told me that I must never, under any circumstances, tell her anything. I assumed he was only referring to the sex, because she must have known how he earned his money.

I had been working as a prostitute for about five years when I found out I had syphilis, with maybe the last two of them under Christoph's control. It's difficult to put all the events into chronological order because I didn't have any real concept of time and no means of measuring it. There was nothing to distinguish the days, weeks, months and years from all the others that had gone before them, or from those that were to follow them. The only thing that could change from one month to the next was the brothel I was working in, which might be in a different town. Even the brothels and, with a few exceptions, the brothel owners were pretty much the same. And so were most of the men who paid a few euros to have five-minute sex with a girl they couldn't have picked out of a line-up of two.

By the time I had been working as a prostitute for five years, I had almost forgotten the life I used to imagine I might have, working as a waitress to earn enough money to put myself through college. After a while, you don't really think about anything, certainly not the future, which you know will be exactly like the present, or worse.

One day, Christoph picked me up from the hotel and drove me to do an 'outcall', an escorting job on the other side of the city. Afterwards, when he was driving me back to the hotel, he stopped the car in a public car park and said, 'We need to talk.'

It felt as though something was squeezing my stomach, making me feel sick and sending a spasm of anxiety throughout my whole body. What had I done wrong? I tried to think of everything that had happened during the last couple of days. And then I realised that Christoph was speaking to me again in a voice that didn't sound angry at all.

'I think you should open a Facebook account,' he said. 'Get in touch with some of your friends back in England. You've proved that you can be trusted. It's time for you to have a bit of freedom in your life and do something nice.'

I had been expecting him to slap me or, at the very least, to shout at me for something I had or hadn't done. So, for the few seconds it took for me to understand what he was saying, I just stared at him. Even when it did sink in, I hardly dared to believe it.

'We'll do it now. Come on.' Christoph smiled and got out of the car, and I walked beside him across the car park, down the street and into an internet café.

When your life is pretty much at rock bottom, you'd think it would take a lot to make you feel happy. For me, it was quite the reverse: even relatively insignificant, inconsequential events seemed exciting. Knowing that Christoph was pleased with me would have been enough to cheer me up; the thought that I was going to be able to make contact with old friends from home made me feel like a child who had just been told that it was Christmas.

In the café, Christoph ordered us each a coffee and then, after he had set up a Facebook account for me, I began to search for people I used to know five years ago. I sent messages to a couple of girls who used to be my friends, asking how they were and what they were doing and saying that I was working in Greece. Then I began to feel anxious again: would anyone answer? It suddenly seemed really important that someone did.

When we were back in the car, Christoph handed me a new phone and said, 'Take it. I think I can trust you now.' I don't know if I thought he meant that he wouldn't check it regularly for texts and to see what calls I made and received, but whatever I thought, I remember that I felt special, and proud to have earned his praise.

We went back to the same café every day for the next three days, so that I could check for messages. I almost cried when I saw that people had posted comments on my Facebook page. And I was really excited when I got an email in response to the message I had sent to a girl called Lexi, who'd been a good friend of mine at school. She said she was really glad I had got in touch at last and she asked me loads of questions, about where I was living and what I was doing. Christoph had put up some of the photographs he took from time to time for me to send my mother, and Lexi said she had barely recognised me and that it looked as though I was having a great time.

Christoph said he was really pleased for me and told me what to say in response to Lexi's message – that I loved living in Athens and was earning a lot of money working in a bar that was very popular with tourists. It was odd: while I was writing Christoph's words, I felt a sort of glow of excitement inside me, as though what I was saying was true.

When Christoph came to pick me up the next day and take me back to the internet café, he asked me, 'Why don't you invite your friend Lexi to come and stay with you for a holiday?' I didn't answer him, because I thought I must have misunderstood what he had said. 'I think you already know that I have feelings for you,' he continued, 'feelings that I don't have for any of the other girls. You're different, special. You've worked hard and you've earned a break. So tell your friend that I'll pay for her flight and that she won't have to worry about money while she's here either.'

I believed every single word of it. I felt proud to be special, happy that Christoph was pleased with me, and almost ecstatic at the prospect of having a friend again, even if it would be for just a few days. When I look back on it now, I almost feel contempt for the gullible, pathetic, easily manipulated girl I was then.

Lexi answered my message immediately, accepting Christoph's invitation, and within a week she was on her way to visit me in Athens.

Her flight arrived in the early hours of the morning and Christoph drove me to the airport to meet her. As I stood at the arrivals gate, waiting for her to come through the door, I felt excited but apprehensive, as though I had stepped outside the reality of my life and into some sort of parallel universe. And then I saw Lexi, waving frantically and almost bouncing with delight. We laughed as we hugged each other, and then I introduced her to 'my friend Christoph', who smiled and charmed her and insisted on carrying her backpack.

Instead of taking us to the hotel I was staying at, as I had assumed he would do, Christoph drove into the city centre and parked outside a house in a narrow street. 'I'm afraid I haven't had a chance to sort out a room in the hotel for your friend,' he said, smiling apologetically at Lexi. 'So I'm going to leave you both here with a friend of mine while I go and do that now. I won't be long.'

As incredible as it seems to me now, I didn't suspect a thing. In fact, it wasn't until the front door of the house was opened by a cheerful Albanian man Christoph introduced to us as Zamir that I felt the first prickle of doubt.

Christoph didn't come into the house with us. He left us on the doorstep, saying he would be back within an hour or so. Lexi and I followed Zamir into the living room, where two more men were sitting watching television and drinking whisky. I suddenly felt anxious and uneasy. But the men were pleasant and friendly, so we took the drinks they offered us and after we had all been chatting for a while, I began to relax.

We were all laughing about something when Lexi stood up and said she needed to go to the toilet. One of the men picked up the remote and turned off the TV. 'Tell her to sit down,' he said, in a very different voice. When I glanced towards him, I saw that he was looking from one to the other of us with an expression of scornful disdain. In that split-second, I realised that I had made a terrible mistake. A voice in my head was shouting, 'No! You idiot! What have you done?' And my whole body began to shake.

Lexi hadn't understood what the man had said, but there was no mistaking the threat in his voice or the suddenly tense atmosphere in the room, and she began to cry.

'You do know what's happened, don't you?' the man asked me. 'You understand what you and your friend will be doing? You belong to us now. We bought you off Christoph, for four thousand euros.' He made a sideways movement with his head to indicate Lexi. 'You'd better explain it to your friend.'

Why was I shocked and hurt at the thought that Christoph had sold me to these men? What possible grounds did I have for believing that a man who treated me like an inanimate commodity actually cared about me and wanted to do something nice for me? The answer, in part, was that I was so desperate to have a friend, my mind had simply blocked out any information that didn't support what I wanted to believe. I had felt guilty and ashamed every day for more than five years, but never as much as I did that day.

You can adapt to almost any new normality, given time, and over the last few years my emotions and reactions had been damped down. But Lexi was used to a more rational, everyday sort of normality, and when I told her what the man had said, she started screaming and running round the room, flailing her arms, bumping into the furniture and sending all the whisky glasses crashing to the floor.

When Zamir's two friends stood up, I raised my arms instinctively to cover my face. But instead of lashing out at us with their fists, as I had expected them to do, one of the men said to Zamir, 'We don't want to do this. They're going to get us into trouble.' Then they walked out of the living room and a few seconds later we heard the front door open and close behind them.

Lexi was still sobbing and shouting when Zamir walked out of the living room too, and I could hear him somewhere at the front of the house, talking rapidly and angrily on his phone. Realising that it would probably be our only opportunity, I snatched up Lexi's backpack and thrust it into her hand, then pulled her with me out of the living room, across the hallway and into a room at the back of the house. I had only just managed to turn the key in the lock when Zamir started kicking the door and screaming threats at us. Lexi was screaming too and I was sobbing. But I knew that if we were going to stand any chance at all of getting out of the house, I had to force myself to think.

There were only two ways into and out of the room we were locked in – through the door that was about to come crashing in on us, and through the window in the wall opposite it. For a few precious seconds, I fumbled with the catch on the window before managing to open it. Then I almost pushed Lexi out of it. As I was climbing out after her, looking over my shoulder and expecting to see Zamir burst into the room behind me, I almost missed my footing and fell. Then my feet touched the ground and we started running.

I don't know what people thought when they saw us, two girls running side by side through the city centre, crying and glancing behind them every few seconds like hunted animals. I didn't have a destination in mind; I was simply following my instinct to get as far away from the house as possible. I thought, as I always did, that someone might be watching me. But we couldn't keep running for ever. So when we rounded a corner and saw a policeman standing at the side of the road, I stopped, with my hand on Lexi's arm, and tried to catch my breath.

'Please help us,' I said as soon as I could speak. As I tried to explain to the policeman what had happened, Lexi kept shouting, in English, 'Help us! We've been kidnapped!'

'You're safe now,' the policeman said when I eventually paused again for breath. 'You had better come with me.' So we followed him across the road into the lobby of a hotel, where he told us to wait while he went outside again to make a phone call.

We sat down in some chairs in a corner of the lobby where we could see the entrance but wouldn't be immediately visible to anyone coming into the hotel. And that's when I suddenly realised that I had been there before. In fact, it was the hotel I had stayed in with Mum when she came to Athens to visit me. I would have been panic-stricken wherever we had been waiting, but one of the last places in the world I wanted to be at that moment was in a hotel that was owned by a friend of Christoph's and where someone might recognise me. Turning slightly in my chair so that I had my back to the reception desk, I let my hair fall forward over my face. I was still trying to decide what to do, if anything, when I saw Christoph.

He had just pushed open the door from the street and was scanning the lobby as if he was looking for someone. I shrank back into my seat and whispered to Lexi to put her head down. But it was too late. Christoph had already seen us and was walking towards us across the brown-tiled floor.

'I'm so sorry,' he said, smiling as he looked, first at Lexi, then at me. 'I had no idea. I can't believe what happened to you. I'm so angry with Zamir. Thank heavens you're both safe. Please, come with me.'

It took a moment for the fact to sink in that rather than being angry with us, he was smiling and apologising. And then it dawned on me that if Christoph knew what had happened to us, *he* must have been the person the police-man had phoned when he had gone outside – which meant that no one was coming to help us.

Chapter 12

Instead of taking us to the hotel I had been staying in, Christoph drove us to an apartment about an hour from the city. He kept saying how angry he was with the three Albanians and telling us we mustn't worry anymore because he would take care of us.

'Stay here,' he said when we arrived at the apartment. 'Don't go out on your own.' He looked at me without expression for a few seconds before adding, 'I'll be back in the morning with some money and to show you around the area. It's a very interesting place. I think you'll like it.'

In fact, he didn't come back the next day, or the day after that. I was now more convinced than ever that someone would always be watching me, and as Lexi and I were too frightened to leave the apartment, we had nothing to eat.

Being hungry was an added stress for Lexi, but I had survived for longer on just tap water. Although we both had phones, neither of us had any credit, and after what had just happened, going to a police station wasn't an option either.

As the hours ticked by, Lexi became more frightened, and I found it increasingly difficult to think of anything even remotely reassuring to say to her. I didn't tell her the truth about Christoph, partly because I knew it would make her panic even more, and partly because it would have meant having to tell her the truth about me too. Stuck in that apartment together, we already had enough problems without Lexi having to process the fact that I had lied to her about my wonderful life in Athens and was a prostitute, and I didn't want to have to deal with the knowledge that she despised me.

I knew there was nothing we could do that would change whatever was going to happen. And Lexi was too scared and confused to argue with me when I said we would just have to wait for Christoph to come back. Ultimately, I was going to pay the price for running away and talking to the policeman. But I didn't believe that Christoph would harm Lexi or even that he had any real intention of trafficking her and making her work as a prostitute. If I was wrong, I would be responsible for whatever happened to her.

We had been in the apartment for three days by the time Christoph came back. He brought with him some clothes for me and some takeaway food, and he apologised, briefly, for having been away so long. Then he told me, coldly, 'You made a very big mistake. Don't ever think about running away again. You and your friend are going to have to earn your keep. So tonight you'll be working in a bar.'

When I told Lexi, she was upset and said she didn't want to do it. And then Christoph suddenly broke into smiles and, in a voice that was now almost jovial, said, 'Tell your friend there's nothing to be worried about. All you have to do is talk to guys who come into the bar and encourage them to buy drinks. You'll earn a percentage of all the money they spend.' I really wanted it to be true and for everything to be all right, but I still felt like Judas when I repeated to Lexi what Christoph had said and she decided that it sounded like fun after all and she would do it.

Christoph left us at the apartment to shower and change, then he came back in the evening to take us to the bar. The bar owner was friendly and after he had given us a brief explanation of the script we were to follow, Lexi and I sat at separate tables and waited.

It was only a few minutes before a man approached Lexi and sat down opposite her. I couldn't hear what they were saying, but he obviously spoke good English, because Lexi was laughing and they seemed to be getting on well.

By the time Christoph picked us up late that night and dropped us back at the apartment, both Lexi and I had done good business for the bar. To Lexi, it had simply been like a game and she was pleased with the way the night had gone. For me, it had been a struggle as I tried to concentrate and listen to what the men were saying to me, because I knew that, at some point, I was going to tell Lexi the truth.

I couldn't pretend to myself any longer that everything would be all right, that Lexi would work in the bar for a few nights and then catch her flight back to England. I had wanted to believe that was what would happen, but in my heart I knew it wasn't and that I had to try to help Lexi before it was too late.

So in reply to her question about when we would get the money we had earned that evening, I told her we wouldn't get any money, that Christoph wasn't 'my friend', but someone who bought and sold girls and made them work as prostitutes, and that everything I had written in my message to her about my life in Greece had been a lie.

She stared at me for what seemed like a long time before saying, very quietly, 'I don't understand.' Then she burst into tears. 'But what if that's what he's planning to make me do?' She sounded frightened and child-like. 'I can't work in a brothel! And you can't stay here either. Oh God, Meg, what are we going to do?'

I was grateful that she didn't turn on me and blame me for the appalling situation she was in – although she didn't have to, because I already blamed myself.

'I know!' She started pulling things out of her backpack. 'That first guy who came into the bar, the guy who stayed so long, he gave me his phone number and a top-up card for *my* phone. I really liked him, Meg. I think we can trust him.'

'I don't think we can trust anyone,' I said. But I knew that if Lexi was going to have any chance at all of getting away, we were going to have to take the risk.

The guy she phoned was an Albanian called Petros, and when she explained, briefly, what had happened and asked him to help us, he said, 'I'll come to the bar again tomorrow evening. When I get there, just do what I tell you and don't ask any questions.'

Neither of us slept much that night. I told Lexi a bit more about the life I had really been living. Then I lay on the bed staring at the ceiling, trying not to think about the trap we might be walking into. Lexi was certain that Petros would help us – as certain as I would have been if I had asked Jak for help when I first met him in a bar five years earlier. My main anxiety, however, was based on my belief that Christoph saw everything. I didn't really think I would ever escape.

We stayed in the apartment throughout the next day, until Christoph came in the evening to take us to the bar. I'm surprised he didn't suspect something was wrong. I had told Lexi several times during the day – until I could see she was starting to get fed up with me – that, whatever happened, we had to act normally and not do anything that might raise Christoph's or anyone else's suspicions. But I was acutely aware as we drove with him to the bar that our silences were tense and our chatter falsely cheerful.

Within minutes of arriving at the bar, a man sat down at Lexi's table. I could see she was trying at least to appear to be concentrating on what he was saying, but she kept inclining her head slightly so that it was obvious to anyone watching her that she was looking past him to the door that led out on to the street. I was trying to think of some way of attracting her attention so that I could warn her when the door opened and Petros walked into the bar.

My heart had already been racing and now I gripped the edge of the table tightly with both hands. This was the moment when we would find out whether Petros really could be trusted or whether he had come back to the bar for the sole purpose of betraying us.

Lexi was sitting at the table next to mine and as Petros passed between us, he said, quietly and without looking at either of us, 'Don't say anything; don't ask me any questions. Just get up, follow me out of the bar and get into my car.'

I had to force myself to do what he had said and not run out ahead of him into the night. It was the same feeling I'd had when I had shoplifted in England, a whole lifetime ago – when I had been certain that the eyes of every single person in the shop were focused on my back, every fibre of my body was telling me to run, and I was just waiting for the moment I knew would come when someone would shout 'Stop!' But no one did try to stop us that night in the bar. And what was even more amazing than that was the fact that Petros had kept his promise and come back for us.

That night, Lexi and I stayed with Petros and his friend in their hotel room. Although the two men gave us their beds, I don't think any of us slept very much. Christoph called my phone almost constantly and sent me texts saying, 'I know where you are. I'm on my way to get you. You and your mum are in BIG trouble.'

With every text, I became more convinced that he had some way of tracking my phone and that he really did know where I was. By the early hours of the morning I was a nervous wreck, but I had come to a decision. 'I've got to leave,' I told Lexi. 'I think Christoph knows where I am and if he comes here, he'll find you too. Even if I'm wrong and he doesn't know that we're here, he'll go after my mum, and I can't let him hurt her. I've got to go back to him.'

'You can't!' Lexi began to cry. 'Please, Meg, there must be some other way. You can't go back to the life he's been making you live. We'll be all right. Petros and his friend will help us. I know we can trust them.'

'I think you're right,' I said. 'But I know Christoph and I know the sort of people he works with. If I don't go back to him, he *will* hurt my mum – or worse. I'm sure Petros will get you a flight home. I've got to go back.'

It was the second time I had tried to imagine what it would be like to be on a flight back to England. The truth is that I couldn't imagine it and I was afraid, in the same way, perhaps, that a wild animal that's been kept in a cage for years would be afraid if you suddenly opened the door and gave it the chance to be free. I thought I had the life that, for some reason, I deserved and that what had happened to me was my fault. It was certainly my fault that Lexi was in Greece and in the position she was in. I didn't want to have to blame myself for something terrible happening to my mum, too. So I hugged Lexi and made Petros promise again that he would take care of her. Then I left the hotel and started walking down a deserted road with my back to the rising sun.

I kept walking along the same road until I was some distance from the hotel, not far from what looked a small farmhouse in the middle of dusty, stony fields, and then I phoned Christoph.

He answered immediately. 'Where are you?' he asked, the cold quietness of his voice more intimidating than angry shouting would have been.

I told him what I could see ahead of me and described various landmarks I had just passed.

'Keep walking, and stay on the phone,' he said.

I must have gone almost another mile by the time he told me to sit down at the side of the road. And that's when I knew he could see me.

'Don't hurt me, please,' I whispered into the phone. 'I'm sorry. Please.'

When his car pulled up beside me, his icy control had given way to screaming fury and he shouted at me to get in. I was crying and shaking so much that I fumbled with the handle for what seemed like an eternity before I finally managed to open the door. As soon as I was inside the car, Christoph hit me across the head with a gun with such force that I thought I was going to pass out.

'Where's the girl?' he shouted, striking me again with the gun and this time knocking me sideways so that the other side of my head smashed against the window. 'Did you really think you could just walk away? Where is she?'

'I don't know,' I sobbed. 'Really, I don't know. She ran off with a man she met at the bar. I don't know where they went. Honestly.'

'I thought I could trust you.' For a moment, I thought he was crying. It was if he had completely lost control, and suddenly I was more afraid of him than I had ever been. 'Why did you run away from me?' he demanded. 'Wait and see what's going to happen to you now! Did you not understand what I told you about your mother? I can get rid of someone just like that.' He snapped his fingers in my face. 'Give me your phone.'

When I handed it to him he took out the SIM card, snapped the phone in two and threw the pieces out of the window.

'Don't fuck with me!' he screamed. 'I'm a very dangerous person. I am going to chop you up into little pieces and bury them.' He reached across the car to where I was cowering against the door and hit me again. Then, as if at the flick of a switch, he stopped shouting and said very quietly, in a voice full of ominous threat, 'I don't care

209

about the girl. The stupid bitch has caused me nothing but trouble since the moment she arrived. And then she tried to steal you away from me.' I had spent five years believing things that couldn't possibly be true, but even I could see that was a bizarre interpretation of what had happened. It was one I was happy to encourage, however, if it meant that Lexi would be safe and it took some of the heat off me.

Christoph didn't take me back to the apartment to pick up my stuff before driving me back to Athens. It wasn't the first time, or the last, that I had to abandon my suitcase and its contents. But it didn't matter; I didn't own anything, so all I lost each time were a few cheap items of clothing, which were easily replaced. When we got back to the city, he took me to a posh hotel, booked a double room and had sex with me. Then he turned on his side and went to sleep.

Living in a world where all the normal rules and expectations don't apply really messes with your head. I wonder now if Christoph – or any of the other men who controlled me at different times during the years I was in Greece – ever did *anything* that was spontaneous and without some underlying purpose. I think the answer's probably no, and that every single thing they said and did was deliberately intended to confuse and destabilise me, so that I no longer knew what 'normal' was. That was certainly what happened. One minute Christoph would be raging at me, saying terrible things; the next minute he would praise me and tell me I was special. Because I couldn't ever predict what his reaction would be and never knew if something I was doing was right or wrong, I became incredibly insecure and full of self-doubt.

He even did it when we were having sex. 'Your legs are closed too much,' he might say. 'Next time, make sure they're that far apart,' and he would indicate the 'right' distance with his arms. Sometimes he would complain that my make-up was all wrong, my hair was a mess, or I was putting on weight – which was certainly never true, because I had no appetite and had to force myself to eat anything at all. I was programmed to believe it all though, and I believed it was my fault that, however hard I tried, I always seemed to get things wrong.

Christoph slept for about an hour in the hotel that day. When he woke up, he gave me my old SIM card and a new phone, put 50 euros on the table beside the bed and told me he would be back the next morning. After he had gone, I went downstairs and spent the money he had given me on alcohol, which I drank alone in the room.

That night, I had a text from Lexi saying that Petros had kept his word and booked a flight for her back to England. 'You should have been on it with me,' she wrote. I read the text maybe 20 times before I deleted it so that Christoph wouldn't find it. Each time I read it, I tried to imagine where I would be and what I would be doing if I hadn't been too afraid to fly back to London with my friend.

I still feel incredibly guilty about what happened to Lexi. I invited her to visit me in Greece because I wanted so badly to believe what Christoph told me. I did what I had done a thousand times before and closed my mind to the possibility that he might have reasons other than the ones he told me about – in this case, that I deserved to have a break with a friend. I had got involved with Jak because my judgement was bad; by the time Lexi came to Athens, it was ten times worse. As a result of my immense stupidity, she came very close to being trapped into becoming a prostitute.

I didn't ever hear from Lexi again. I'm sure that when she thought about it, she did blame me for what almost happened to her. I know I blame myself. Despite what I told her, she must have thought I really had chosen the life I was leading; otherwise, I would have escaped with her. In a way, she would have been right, because although I didn't *choose* it, I had learned to accept it because I didn't think I deserved anything better.

Lexi had a 'normal' reaction to fear: she tried to get away. So it would have been difficult for her to understand why I didn't. But there's another type of fear that perhaps you can only understand if you've experienced it. It's a fear of nothing and of everything, of things real and imagined, and it's so overwhelming that it prevents you doing anything except what you've been told to do.

When Christoph came the next day, he took me to an apartment that, although pretty basic, was quite spacious compared with all the other places I had stayed. There was a small living room with a bed and sliding doors that opened on to a tiny balcony, an even smaller bedroom, a bathroom and a galley kitchen with just enough room for a sink, a cooker and a filthy, mould-encrusted, under-the-counter fridge. I had lived off takeaways for the last five years, and I really liked the idea of being able to cook for myself. So, after I had dropped off my bag at the apartment, Christoph took me to a supermarket and bought me some food.

Once again, the only thing that had changed was the place I slept. Everything else continued pretty much in the same way it had done before. Christoph picked me up every morning, took me to a brothel or to do escort jobs, and then dropped me off again in the early hours of the next day. The fact that I'd had syphilis didn't seem to matter from any practical point of view, except that now all the men that had sex with me had to wear condoms. When I wasn't working, I was in the apartment, with nothing to do except sleep or eat. In fact, the only thing that ever varied from day to day was the way Christoph treated me. Sometimes, he would arrive at the apartment and, without any warning or apparent reason, start punching me in the head. Or he would grab me by the neck, lift my feet off the floor and slam me against the wall, shouting into my face, 'Your time's running out now. You're not earning enough money. You need to start acting more innocent. What's the matter with you? You're like a smackhead. Men want fresh meat and you're getting old.' I was 19; I felt much older, and incredibly tired.

One day, after Christoph had been shouting at me and punching me repeatedly until my ear had begun to bleed, he got some scissors from the kitchen and cut up all my clothes. Then he grabbed a handful of my hair, yanking my head to one side so sharply it felt as though my neck was going to snap, and cut out all my hair extensions.

Later, when he had calmed down, he took me to get my hair cut properly. He told the hairdresser he was my dad and that I had thrown a bit of a wobbly and hacked at it myself. 'I'll come back for her in about an hour,' he said, patting my shoulder and raising his eyebrows at her as if to say, 'What is she like?' I felt really embarrassed, like some spoilt brat of a girl who'd had a tantrum. And although I spoke Greek well by that time, the hairdresser could tell that I wasn't actually Greek. So I don't know what she thought.

When someone shouts at you and is violent, and you just have to stand there and take it because you can't turn away and there's nowhere to hide, you feel like a very frightened, vulnerable child. The worst thing of all, though, was knowing that Christoph was right and I was no longer 'good enough' to be a prostitute in a sleazy brothel. And if I wasn't good enough for that, what *was* I good enough for?

One evening when I had my period and wasn't working, Christoph came to the apartment anyway. As soon as I had closed the front door behind him, he started slapping me and shouting really horrible things. Then, suddenly, he stopped, turned around and stormed out again.

After he had left, I stayed on my knees on the floor and cried in a way that was different from all the ways I had cried before. I think it was the first time I had ever felt so upset purely for my own sake. I was having flashbacks to everything that had happened since I had come to Athens almost six years earlier – years that I now realised I was never going to get back, but that would colour my life for ever.

There had been a few items of cheap clothing and a bottle of vodka in the apartment when I moved in. I often wondered what had happened to the girl who had left them there, and I thought about her again now. Was she going through the same experiences I was? Did *anyone* else feel the way I did? I sometimes felt as though I was living in some kind of parallel universe that had always existed alongside the one I had lived in as a child and where the things I was doing were normal. I could hear Christoph's voice in my head saying, 'Men want fresh meat and you're getting old.' Like any young person, I couldn't imagine myself actually being old, but it did make me wonder what would happen to me when men didn't want to have sex with me at all and I was no longer any use to Christoph. The present was frightening; the future seemed even more so.

I thought about my mum a hundred times every day, and I thought about her then, as I was kneeling on the floor, crying like someone bereaved. I felt more alone and more in despair than I had felt at any other time during all the lonely, desperate years I had been in Greece. And then

I remembered the bottle of vodka that had been left in a kitchen cupboard, presumably by the previous occupant of the apartment.

I started drinking it straight from the bottle, but it was so strong and foul-tasting it made me retch. So I poured some into a glass and added water, which enabled me to drink it quickly without being sick. I found some painkillers in the kitchen too, and swallowed all of them. Then I stumbled into the bathroom and looked at myself in the mirrored door of the cabinet on the wall.

'I hate you,' I screamed at my reflection. 'You're nothing. Nobody cares about you. Nobody loves you. Why are you still here? You don't deserve to be alive.'

But only the coldest, blackest-hearted person could really have hated the pathetic, pitiable girl who was looking back at me from the mirror. As all the anger and frustration drained out of me as I reached out my hand to touch her swollen face and then opened the door of the cabinet to make her disappear.

Amongst the few discarded items on the shelves inside was a razor. When I touched its handle, the anger returned and as I ran back into the kitchen, I began to slash at my wrists and neck with its blade. I started cutting my arms, then my legs, and before long there was blood everywhere, on my body, soaking into my clothes, splashed on the walls and dripping on to the floor.

I don't know what it was specifically that made me pass out; it could have been the alcohol, the tablets, stress caused by my manic episode, blood loss, or a combination of all four. I collapsed next to the open glass door that led out on to the balcony. The neighbours had heard me shouting and crashing around the apartment, and when they saw me slumped on the floor covered in blood, they called the police.

It must have been the sound of the front door being kicked in that woke me up. I came to slowly, like a diver rising up from the depths of the ocean, and at first I was disorientated and couldn't remember what had happened. I heard the sound of running footsteps and voices shouting 'Police!', and suddenly the living room seemed to be full of men with guns. Somehow, I managed to get to my feet and out on to the balcony, where I tried to throw myself over the railing that surrounded it.

The apartment was on the fifth floor and I would certainly have been killed if two of the policemen hadn't managed to grab hold of my legs just as my stomach hit the metal rail. But I didn't want to be saved, so I struggled and tried to fight them off. I was still kicking and swearing at them when they put the handcuffs on me. And as they walked with me out of the building, I started shouting, 'He's still watching me. I know he's here. He won't stop until he gets me. He's got other girls, you know. He's going to kill me.'

'Who's watching you?' one of the policemen asked me. 'Who's going to kill you?'

'The man,' I told him. 'There's a horrible man. I won't say his name.'

217

I only dared mention Christoph's existence at all because I was drunk. So perhaps it was also the vodka that suddenly made me realise that I was incredibly tired of always being afraid. To the policemen, I must have sounded like every other paranoid drunk they had ever had to deal with.

At the police station, someone cleaned me up, bandaged the worst lacerations on my arms, and asked what had happened to me. 'I cut myself,' I told him. Then I laughed like someone who had lost her mind. In fact, the policemen gave me coffee and were nice to me. They even let me go outside to smoke a cigarette, although the policeman who came with me didn't hesitate to draw his gun when I tried to run away, and I heard a click as he released the safety catch.

When they asked me for my passport, I told them, 'It's probably in the apartment somewhere. Oh no, wait a minute, I think I threw it in the bin.' I laughed again, as though I had made a really funny joke.

'Well, we're going to have to look for it there then,' one of the policemen said. But I knew they would never find it, because Christoph had it.

For the next few hours, I sat in the police station, drinking coffee and staring into space, my mind completely empty of any thoughts. By the time they finally took me out and put me in another car, the anaesthetic effect of the vodka was wearing off and I was starting to feel sick.

'We're going to take you to the hospital,' one of the policemen told me. And even in my confused, drunken state, I could see that that was probably a good idea: I didn't want to get blood poisoning from someone else's discarded razor to add to all my other problems. I wouldn't have got into the police car as willingly as I did, however, if I had known where they were really going to take me.

Chapter 13

The car stopped at the main entrance to a dilapidated-looking brick building. When the two police officers took me inside, I sat in an office, still handcuffed, while a man asked me lots of questions. Had I ever tried to do this sort of thing before? Where did I come from? Did I have family in Greece? What job did I do?

'I'm a prostitute,' I told him. This time, I wasn't sure if the loud, manic laugh really did come from me, although when I looked closely at the man and the nurse who was standing beside him, they didn't seem to be laughing at all. 'I'm only joking,' I said. 'I'm a waitress really. I've been missing my family and friends. I suppose everything just got on top of me.' I think I told him that I couldn't cope anymore and that all I wanted to do was die. Mostly, though, I doubt whether my answers to his questions made much sense, and some of them were totally untrue.

Eventually, the man stood up, nodded at the nurse and said, 'Right, well, first of all we need to have a look at those cuts and get them cleaned up.'

The nurse took me into another room, where she dabbed brown liquid on the broken skin of my arms, legs, face, neck, chest and breasts, and then re-bandaged the worst of it.

'Great. Okay,' I said when she had finished. 'Well, I'm all right to go now then, am I?' When she didn't answer, I turned to the two policemen. But they didn't say anything either. They just looked at the nurse, one of them wished me good luck, and then they walked out of the room.

My cockiness – which was part alcohol induced, part faked bravado, part mental breakdown – evaporated instantly and I shouted, 'Hey! Wait! Where are you going? What's going on?' I was about to follow the policemen when two men in white coats appeared in the doorway and stuck a needle in my arm.

I think I kept on screaming and shouting for another few seconds, although it might just have been in my head. Then all the muscles in my body seemed to relax. I tried to concentrate on sending a message from my brain to my legs, but nothing happened; so I glanced down quickly to make sure they were still there, and then laughed, in embarrassment this time.

Someone helped me on to a bed. Perhaps it was the same person who tied my arms to its railings with thick bands of leather. I couldn't see anyone clearly by that time, because my head was full of swirling white fog and my eyes wouldn't focus.

I remember lying on my back looking up at the lights in the ceiling and wondering why they were moving. And then I was in a room, still lying on the bed, and there was another girl sitting on another bed with her arms clasped around her knees, rocking slowly backwards and forwards. The girl didn't look at me, and for a while I lay there watching her. Eventually I asked her, 'What are you doing? Why are you in here?' And the sound of my voice made me laugh because it was deep and croaky, not like my real voice at all, and it seemed to echo inside my head. Again, maybe I didn't actually say the words out loud, because the girl kept rocking backwards and forwards and didn't answer.

'I've got a knife,' I shouted, to what was probably an empty corridor outside the open door of the room. 'I'd hidden it in my shirt. I'm going to stab myself with it. Uh-oh, I'm doing it now.'

I didn't have a knife of course, and as my arms were still tied to the head of the bed, I couldn't have done anything with it if I had. I just wanted someone to come into the room so that I could tell them … I don't know what I wanted to tell them. It didn't matter anyway, because no one did come. But I didn't give up: I kept on shouting until I lost my voice and thought I was about to die of thirst. All the time, the girl kept rocking. And still no one came.

I must have fallen asleep eventually. When I woke up, there was light streaming in through a barred window and I felt almost calm. I hadn't been awake very long when a nurse came in, unstrapped my wrists and asked me if I would like to have a shower. I felt better when I was clean, although for some reason I couldn't stop crying. The nurse sat on the bed beside me and talked to me in a kind, gentle way. Then she took me to the canteen, where, despite having eaten nothing for at least 24 hours, I only managed to drink some orange juice.

I was heavily medicated, so everything that happened during the next few days is all jumbled up in my mind. I know that at some point, maybe after breakfast on that first morning, the nurse took me out for a walk around the vast hospital grounds. Beyond the grass that surrounded the building there was a small forest, and beyond the forest were two huge gates flanked on either side by a very high wall topped with barbed wire and numerous cameras. I think it was seeing those gates that finally made me under-stand that I had been sectioned and was in a mental hospital.

During that first day, I was taken by another nurse back to the office I had been in the previous day, where I was asked more questions by a man who turned out to be the hospital's chief psychiatrist. Paradoxically – considering I

223

had almost killed myself and was an in-patient in a psychiatric hospital in a foreign country – all I was really worried about was what I had shouted as I was leaving the apartment building with the police. I knew I had said something about Christoph, but I couldn't remember if I had said his name. I kept wondering if he had been watching from somewhere in the shadows and had heard whatever it was I said.

I think I spent most of the rest of that day lying on my bed, moping and recovering from all the alcohol I had drunk the day before. At some point, after I had seen the psychiatrist, I was given all the things that had been in my bag when the police found me, and it wasn't long before my phone rang.

'Where are you?' Christoph sounded angry. 'The woman I rent the apartment from says you caused trouble and that she won't rent it to me anymore. What did you do? What's going on?'

'I got drunk,' I told him, in a sad little girl's voice. 'I'm sorry. I was stupid. I cut myself, on purpose, so the police arrested me and now I'm in a hospital.'

I waited for his anger to explode. But when he spoke again his tone had changed completely. 'Why, baby?' he asked. 'I'm so upset that you've done something like that to yourself. Why would you do that? What's going on?'

'I'm sorry,' I whispered again.

'What have you told them at the hospital?' There was a hard edge to his voice.

'They think I've got "issues"', I told him. 'They've put me on medication and they say I need some help.'

'I think they're right, baby.' He was solicitous again now. 'I think you've been struggling for the last few weeks. I noticed it and now I wish I had taken you to the hospital myself. Am I allowed to visit you?'

I told him I would ask and, very gently, without my being aware of it, he began to close the trap around me again.

Visiting hours at the hospital were flexible and when Christoph came the following day, he was almost invisible behind a huge bunch of flowers, and he was carrying in his other hand a bag full of nice things to eat and drink. I told the hospital staff he was a friend, someone who looked after me, and he went out of his way to be polite and charming to them. Despite everything, I couldn't help being pleased to see him.

Patients and their visitors could go into a sitting room or walk around the grounds. Christoph came with me to my room first, while I put away the things he had brought for me. My roommate – the girl with empty eyes who spent hours every day in perpetual rocking motion – wasn't there. So there was no one except me to see Christoph touch my arm or hear him say, 'You have no idea how much I miss fucking you. I can't wait until things are back to normal. I'm going to get you a lovely apartment when you're better. I think it's time you had a rest. Maybe you should have a holiday. Don't worry, my girl. I'll sort it out.'

Christoph often called me 'my girl' and I liked it. I had always wanted to be someone's girl. I had thought for a while I was Jak's and had felt special because of it. When I was very young, I used to think I was my dad's girl, before things changed and he seemed to stop caring about everything and everyone else. It's funny how something so simple mattered so much to me. Being called 'my girl' by Christoph had been one of the reasons why I had fooled myself into believing he had real feelings for me. Among the other reasons were self-deception fuelled by emotional neediness and the fact that I had absolutely no judgement about men or relationships.

Christoph's quiet, soothing tone didn't alter as he added, 'If you say anything about what you've been doing, no one will believe you. They'll think you're crazy, and they'll keep you in here for ever. If by any chance they did believe you and I got into trouble because of something you had said, you would have signed your own death warrant – and your mother's too.' It was little wonder that I was always confused and uncertain.

I was put on several different types of medication while I was in the hospital, including an antidepressant, a drug to boost the antidepressant, and another drug to help reduce anxiety. I also had daily assessment sessions with the psychiatrist. I didn't ever talk about Christoph or anything that had happened to me during what was now the last six years. But I began to think that the psychiatrist knew. As the days merged into weeks, he often told me I was making good progress. Then, one day, he said, 'I don't think you really want to kill yourself, do you, Megan? I think you had a specific reason for doing what you did. If you need our help, we can protect you, you know.'

He was a nice man, and although I didn't believe that, ultimately, he really would be able to protect me from Christoph, I knew that his good intentions were genuine. In fact, strange as it may seem, I actually liked being in the hospital. I felt safe there, for the first time in years. It was like being inside an impenetrable but invisible bubble: I could take part in whatever was going on around me while at the same time remaining cushioned and protected. Something else I liked about being there was the fact that I made friends and had people to talk to.

There was one old lady I became particularly close to. She was usually sweet and friendly, and then sometimes when you tried to talk to her she would tell you to 'eff off'. She was never aggressive or vicious though, and it just made everyone laugh. One day, she gave me a box with a pink bow tied round it. I thought at first when I lifted the lid that it was full of cotton wool. Then I saw the silver cross. 'It's for you,' the old lady said. 'It's a present. I want you to have it.' She gave me a card too, in which she had written 'Good luck' in Greek. I've still got them both – the silver cross and the card; they're two of my most treasured possessions.

Perhaps it's only after you've been starved of human contact for a while that you realise just how important it is

227

to be able to interact with other people. Since Jak had left me in Athens, I had only rarely had even the sort of mundane conversations you have with people in shops. I had worked alone in brothels most of the time, and then gone back to a hotel room or an apartment, where I had been on my own again. During the years, the loneliness had built up inside me until it was like something solid. It was at least partly because of that loneliness and aloneness that I had become so dependent on Christoph, and why I was now so grateful for the fact that everyone at the hospital was kind to me.

Christoph visited me almost every other day. We would walk around the grounds and he would talk about the apartment he was going to get for me and how everything was going to be different when I was better. He always repeated his warning too, about what would happen if I told anyone the truth – although he didn't use the word 'truth', of course.

Despite feeling safe in the hospital, I always had the thought that I wasn't going to be able to stay for ever at the back of my mind as I began to get better. After I had been there for almost three months, I was lying on my bed one morning, crying and praying that something would happen to get me out of the mess I was trapped in, when a nurse came into my room. I didn't know she was there until she sat down on the bed beside me, took hold of my hand and said, 'I know, Megan. And it's going to be okay.'

When I went for my session with the psychiatrist the next day, he asked me all the usual questions, told me he was very pleased with the progress I had made, and then said, 'I don't know exactly what's been going on; what I *do* know is that you're in trouble. I'm not going to ask you to talk about things you don't want to talk about, but we want to help you. You understand that, don't you?'

He handed me a tissue, and after I had wiped away my tears, I nodded my head.

'Okay,' he said. 'So just answer yes or no to this question: do you need our help?'

'Yes,' I whispered.

'Good.' He sounded genuinely relieved. 'Well, you need to leave Greece. It isn't safe for you to stay here. Is there anyone in England who could look after you?'

He already knew my mum lived with Nikos on the coast. 'I've got grandparents in England,' I told him. 'They live near London. I don't know their phone number, but Mum will have it. They would take care of me; I'm sure they would.' As I said it, an image flashed into my mind of me as a little girl sitting at the kitchen table in my grand-parents' house, looking at a book with my grandfather. I think I had accepted the fact that I wouldn't ever see him or my grandmother again. And now, suddenly, it was a possibility I was desperate to cling to.

'Right. In that case, I need to speak to your mother first.' He pressed the heels of his hands on to the desk for a moment, then reached for the phone.

For as long as I can remember, certainly ever since I was a very little girl, my body's reaction to extreme anxiety has been to shake. It's quite embarrassing sometimes, because it isn't just gentle shuddering; it's quite noticeable, and totally beyond my control. I was shaking as I sat listening to the doctor talk to my mum, because I knew that something had been set in motion that could make everything either better or considerably worse than it had ever been.

When I was admitted to the hospital, I hadn't wanted Mum to know what had happened, so I had asked them not to contact her. It hadn't been difficult keeping up the pretence – in texts and occasionally phone calls – that everything was going well for me, particularly once I had begun to feel safe at the hospital. After all, I had managed it when I wasn't safe and was working as a prostitute. So I knew it was going to be a huge shock for Mum to hear the truth now. In fact, all the doctor told her was that I had been sectioned after trying to take my own life and that he believed me to be in great danger in Athens. Mum obviously couldn't take in what he was saying at first and he had to repeat some of it and keep reassuring her that I was all right.

When she finally accepted what he was telling her, the doctor said, 'Your daughter says she has grandparents in England who would look after her. If we let her leave the hospital and can get her to where you are, would you be willing and able to take her back to England?' Mum must have said she would. 'In that case,' the doctor continued, 'I need to speak to Megan's grandparents. So if you could let me have their phone number …'

Before he hung up the phone, I talked to my mum too, just to tell her that I really was okay and that I would explain everything when I saw her. Then, after the doctor had spoken to my grandfather and told him much the same thing as he had told my mother, he handed the phone to me again. Although I had learned long ago to hold back the tears when I spoke to my mum, I hadn't heard my granddad's voice for years, and I was crying so much I doubt whether he could understand most of what I was saying. It must have been even more of a shock for him than for my mum, getting a phone call like that out of the blue. He sounded bemused, but kept reassuring me – as he had already assured the doctor – that he and my grandmother would do whatever was required to help me when I got back to England.

Later that same day, one of the nurses told me, 'We're going to need your passport. Do you know where it is?'

'It's in the apartment I was staying in,' I lied. 'I could ask my friend to pick it up and bring it with him next time he comes.'

'That's a good idea,' she said, and although her expression didn't change, I don't think she was fooled for a moment.

When Christoph phoned, I asked him to bring in my passport when he visited me the next day. 'The people at the hospital are asking for it,' I said. 'They need it for my records. I told them it was in the apartment and that I would ask you to bring it in.'

'Why didn't you say you had lost it?' he demanded angrily. 'For God's sake, Megan, do you never learn anything?' But he must have realised it was already too late and that failing to produce it now might lead to questions and complications that, from his point of view, were best avoided. 'I'll bring it tomorrow,' he said, forcing himself to speak pleasantly again. 'And I'll bring some nice food for you as well.'

When Christoph came to see me the next day, we walked around the grounds, as we had done many times before on all the occasions when it had been nice just to have a visitor. This time, though, I couldn't wait for him to leave. The nurses were as coolly polite to him as they always were, but my paranoia seemed to have gone into overdrive and I kept thinking, 'What if he can read my thoughts?' So when he told me he was going to be busy and wouldn't be able to come to see me again for a couple of days, my immediate thought was that it was a trick and he just wanted to see how I would react. Fortunately, I managed to answer him calmly – thanks, in part at least, to the tablets I was taking.

It seems ridiculous now to say that I had mixed feelings as I stood in the hallway and watched Christoph walk away that day. When he stopped in the doorway and turned around to wave, I had to hold my breath to stop myself bursting into tears. As soon as he had gone, I gave my passport to one of the hospital staff.

The next morning, a nurse helped me to pack my bag with the few items of clothing Christoph had brought in for me over the last few weeks. Odd though it may sound, I was very sad to be leaving the hospital. In the three months I had spent there, not a single person had said anything harsh, critical or unkind to me. (Being told to 'eff off' by the old lady didn't count, because there was never any malice in it when she said it and I knew she didn't mean it.) I didn't know what was going to happen next, and the thought of being on the other side of the wall that surrounded the hospital grounds and kept everything inside it safe was very daunting and frightening.

Later that morning, a nurse and a male member of the hospital staff took me by car to the coach station in the centre of Athens, where they bought me a ticket to the coastal town where my mother lived with Nikos. Even though they stood close beside me all the time, I couldn't stop myself looking round nervously every few seconds, expecting to see Christoph's face amongst the crowd, or someone else watching me, waiting to see which coach I got on.

Then my coach was there with its door open and it was time for me to leave. I cried as the nurse hugged me and wished me good luck. 'This is for you,' she said, handing me a bracelet. 'The symbol on it is a Turkish eye. It's supposed to ward off evil. Be safe, Megan. And may God protect you.' If I hadn't known that my mum would be waiting for me at the end of my journey, I don't know if I would have been able to get on the coach. But I did get on it, and as I sat waiting for the driver to close the door and start the engine, I tried to concentrate on taking one breath after another and suppressing the panic that was threatening to engulf me.

I had been dreading the long journey from Athens to the coast, and it was every bit as bad as I had imagined it would be. I couldn't relax, even for a moment. I flinched every time someone passed me on their way down the aisle to use the toilet at the back of the bus, and had to force myself not to keep turning round to see if any of the other passengers were looking at me. And then I began to worry in case the tablets I was taking might have stopped working, and my paranoia would just keep building up and up until it tipped me over the edge into some sort of manic episode.

I had thought for a long time that I was suffering from paranoia – even before I tried to kill myself and ended up in a mental hospital. In fact, I continued to think so until fairly recently, when I looked it up. One of the definitions for the word paranoia is 'an irrational or delusional thought process', another is 'the belief that other people are trying to do you harm even though there's no convincing evidence that that is the case', and another 'the unfounded fear that something bad is going to happen and that other people are responsible for this'. So perhaps it never really was paranoia after all, because most of my fears weren't delusional or unfounded. When you've been physically and mentally abused on a daily basis for years, there's plenty of 'convincing evidence' that people are trying to do you harm, which means that the fears I had were perfectly rational. It's some small comfort, I suppose.

As I sat on the coach that day, I felt excited as well as anxious and frightened, because I was going to see my mum again, for only the second time in six long years. It was after midnight when the coach turned into the station. I saw Mum as soon as the door opened, and I stumbled down the steps, dropped my bag on the ground and ran towards her. We were both crying as we threw our arms around each other. Then Mum held me away from her so that she could look at me, and I could tell that she was shocked and upset by what she saw. 'What happened to you?' she asked me. 'I don't understand, Megan. I thought you were doing so well in Athens. I thought you were happy. Come on, let's go home.'

As we walked together through the almost-deserted streets to the apartment she lived in with Nikos, she asked me again, 'What *happened* to you. Megan?' But what could I tell her when I didn't really understand it myself? Even then, I was still clinging to the belief that Jak had loved me and that, in some inexplicable way, everything that had occurred had been the result of a horrible mistake and not what he had intended when I was 14 years old and we had first gone to Athens together.

Nikos was waiting for us when we arrived at the apartment. He looked strained and anxious, and as he put his arms around me he began to cry. I had tried so many times to imagine what my life might have been like during those lost years if I had stayed in that little town on the coast, close to Mum and Nikos. Now that I was back there, I kept thinking I might suddenly wake up and find that I wasn't.

All Mum and Nikos knew was what the doctor had told Mum on the phone – that I had tried to kill myself and that they had been treating me for anxiety and depression. I hadn't slept on the coach for more than a few minutes at a time and I was exhausted. So we didn't talk much that night. What I did tell them, though, was that from the time I had moved to Athens with Jak, I had been working as a prostitute.

'But the photographs ...' Mum crossed her arms, hugging herself tightly, and bent forward for a moment. 'You were always smiling in the photographs,' she said, sitting upright again. 'You looked so happy.'

'They were all faked,' I told her.

It was really difficult telling them the truth. For six years they had believed that I had made a success of my life in Athens and I hated disappointing them – and humiliating myself. I think Mum was so shocked by what I was saying that she couldn't really take it in. Nikos understood it though, and he put his head in his hands and sobbed. Then suddenly he stood up, sending the little coffee table skidding across the tiled floor, and shouted angrily, 'Jak did this thing to you! He comes to my bar and talks to me like a friend knowing what he has done to you!'

It wasn't until much later, when Mum and I were back in England, that I told her more specifically about some of the things that had happened in Athens. What I did tell her and Nikos, though, was that I had been arrested with Christoph and had been too afraid to admit the truth when the judge asked me if I had been trafficked.

'Oh my God, Megan!' The colour drained out of Mum's face and I thought she was going to pass out. 'We saw something about it on the news, didn't we, Nikos?' Nikos nodded and closed his eyes. 'I can't bear to think about it,' Mum said. 'We were sitting here watching the television while you were living a nightmare that was being reported on the news.'

The next morning, I took the SIM card out of my phone and threw the handset in a bin at the side of the road. I don't know why I kept the SIM card. I think in some weird, mixed-up way I still had feelings for Christoph and that, despite everything, I was reluctant to cut my last remaining connection with him. It's difficult to explain, even to myself. But, again, I think it was at least partly because I didn't want to accept the fact that I had never meant anything to Christoph either. It's hurtful under any circumstances to have to face the fact that someone you've cared about never cared about you. It's even worse to have to accept that you were nothing more to them than a commodity to be bought, sold and disposed of without a backward glance as soon as you had outgrown your financial usefulness.

Mum cried when I told her I'd had syphilis; and she was angry when I described how, one day in the car, Christoph had shown me a photograph of her standing laughing in Nikos's bar and had threatened to kill her if I ever gave him away.

'I wish he *had* come after me,' she said. 'If I had known what he was doing to you, I might have killed him with my own hands. If he thinks I'm afraid of him, he can think again.' It was nice that Mum wanted to protect me, but if she had known, as I did, what Christoph was capable of, she would have known that if he ever did come looking for us, we wouldn't stand a chance.

Although I was taking the tablets they had given me at the hospital, I still jumped at the sound of every backfiring car, banging door and raised voice. I hadn't realised until I was among people again just how scared I had learned to be. Mum tried to make the few days before I left Greece as pleasant as possible for me, but I felt as though I didn't fit into normal society anymore. I was ill at ease all the time – when we were buying food in the supermarket, sitting in a café drinking coffee, or walking along the road in broad daylight surrounded by other people. Whatever we were doing, I couldn't ever rid myself of the feeling that we were being watched and followed.

I wasn't just anxious because I was afraid that Christoph would send someone to find me and take me back to

Athens. I kept thinking about Jak too. And when I had been staying with Mum and Nikos for three days, I saw him coming out of a local supermarket. Mum and I were weaving our way into the shop between bins of brightly coloured beach balls and racks of postcards, and she didn't notice him. When he saw me and beckoned me over, I hung back and let her go in without me.

'Where have you been?' Jak took hold of my hand. 'I couldn't contact you. I tried everything.' He began to cry. 'I sent people to look for you. What's been going on, Megan?'

I don't know if it was his tears that tipped the balance, or if I would have believed him whatever he had said or done; because I did desperately want what he told me to be true. I was elated at the thought that he had been searching for me and that he hadn't meant to leave me alone in Athens to be used and abused as a prostitute for all those years. So when he tore off the corner of his newspaper, wrote his phone number on it and held it out to me, I reached out my hand to take it and promised to text him later that day. Then I breathed deeply a few times to try to control my nervous excitement and went into the shop to find Mum.

Back at the apartment, I asked Nikos to lend me a phone. As soon as I put my SIM card into it, it began to ring. The call was from Christoph's number, as were all the dozens of other missed calls and texts that came flooding in. I didn't answer it, of course, and he kept on ringing and sending messages while I was writing a text to Jak. Jak sent a text back to me almost immediately, asking me to meet him half an hour later outside the shop where I had seen him earlier.

I hadn't told Mum much about the men who had trafficked me, so I think she understood even less than I did that they were ruthless criminals who made huge sums of money out of buying and selling human beings. If she had known, she would have felt quite differently when I told her I was going to go out for a walk. As it was, I think she saw it as a sign that I was starting to regain some self-confidence and she was pleased.

I should have told her the truth. The fact that I didn't must have meant that I knew she would try to stop me. It's hard to believe when I think about it now that, after everything that had happened to me during the last six years, I had apparently learned almost nothing.

Chapter 14

Jak was waiting for me outside the supermarket. He was sitting behind the steering wheel of a brand new car, so I didn't see him at first, because I had expected him to be on his old motorcycle, or another one like it. He leaned across the front passenger seat and pushed the door open for me, and I sat beside him as he drove along the road that curved down to the sea.

He stopped at the bottom of the hill and it wasn't until we had got out of the car that I realised we were looking out across the beach where we used to sit with his friends when I first met him. The sun was quite low in the sky, almost at our eye level, and it looked as though the surface of the water was covered with thousands of tiny, constantly moving mirrors.

I could hear a motorbike engine in the distance and as it got closer I recognised its distinctive rattling sound. 'Quick, get back in the car,' I said urgently to Jak. 'I can't be seen with you.' I was still trying to open the passenger door when Nikos came round the corner on his ancient Mego motorcycle. I ducked down, but I didn't know whether he had seen me and my heart was racing as Jak sped off along the road away from him.

'You'll have to take me back to the shop,' I said. 'We can't see each other again. Mum and Nikos blame you for everything that happened to me. I blamed you too, but …' I didn't finish the sentence and Jak didn't seem to notice my hesitation. As he drove me back to the shop, he talked cheerfully about the house he had built for himself – the fulfilment of a long-held ambition, he said, as though it was a dream I had never shared.

When I was getting out of the car, he took hold of my hand and said, 'Keep in touch, Megan. You know how much I love you, don't you? I'm so sorry for what happened to you. I didn't know anything about it, I promise. I didn't receive a single euro of the money you were earning.'

I watched him drive away. Then I went into the supermarket and bought a large bottle of cheap retsina, which I buried at the bottom of my bag.

Mum and Nikos were waiting for me back at the apartment.

'What have you been doing?' Mum demanded as soon as I walked through the door.

'I saw you!' Nikos was close to tears. 'I saw you with him! I tried to follow you but he drove too fast. Why didn't you come with me, on my bike?'

'What is *wrong* with you, Megan?' Mum sounded distraught. 'Why in God's name would you go back to him?'

'Just leave me alone,' I shouted at them. 'You don't know *anything*. None of it was Jak's fault. But I'm not going to see him again, so you needn't worry.'

'Oh, Megan!' My righteous indignation faltered a bit when I saw the pain in Mum's eyes, and even more when Nikos added, in a low, anguished voice, 'I wish you were flying back to England today, so that I could know you were safe.'

I didn't want to talk about it; I didn't want to think about Jak's house, or his expensive car, or the fact that the crooked, discoloured teeth he had never been able to afford to get fixed were now perfectly even and white. I went into the room that was serving as a makeshift bedroom for me, sat down on the bed and opened the bottle of retsina.

I drank it straight from the bottle, hiding it away in my bag again after every swig. I must have been a quarter of the way through it and was just lifting it to my lips again when Mum walked into the room. She had started to say something as she was opening the door, and when she realised what I was doing she just stood there, open mouthed, for a few seconds. Then, suddenly, she went ballistic and started shouting at me, 'What are you doing?

You can't start drinking! Is that what you're planning to do, turn to drink in the hope that it will solve all your problems?' She snatched the bottle out of my hands, splashing wine over the bedclothes.

Her fury evaporated as quickly as it had come, and as she sank down on to the bed beside me, she said, 'Please, Megan. Please don't do this. It isn't the answer. You know that, don't you?' She sounded weary and despairing, and then anxious as she added, 'Nikos mustn't know about this. He's already worried to death about you. He blames himself for not knowing what Jak is. If he thought you were turning to drink, it would break his heart.'

That night, Mum and I walked together down to the seafront, where we sat outside a café and ate ice-cream. I had been barely aware of the two guys sitting at the table next to ours, until one of them leaned across and said in Albanian, 'Megan? It's you, isn't it? Hi!' His name was Vasos; he was married to one of Jak's cousins and I had met him – and liked him – when I was living with Jak's parents.

'You look so different,' he said. 'But of course it must be years since I last saw you. Did you go back to England? What have you been up to all this time?'

I don't know if he knew. I think now that he probably did. But instead of answering his question, I asked him about Jak and what he had been doing while I'd been away.

'Oh, just working and getting on with his new life.' He shrugged his shoulders and looked uncomfortable. 'You know how it is.'

'What's his new life like?' I asked. 'Has he got anyone … a girlfriend?'

Vasos shrugged again and looked away.

'It's okay.' I tried to sound as though it didn't matter. 'You can tell me. I just want to know what's going on.'

Perhaps he really was a nice guy; I don't know what reason he would have had for telling me the truth, other than sympathy because he could see that I was upset.

'Jak's married,' Vasos said. 'He saved up a lot of money so that he and his wife could have a good life together.'

We were speaking in Albanian, so Mum didn't understand what we were saying. But the hurt that felt like a sharp physical pain must have been clearly visible on my face and she quickly hustled me away.

I don't know whether Vasos was trying to make sure I understood that anything there might have been in the past between me and Jak was now over. It certainly would have taken someone even more delusional than I was to have persisted in believing that Jak had ever loved me. It was the first time I had really faced the truth: while I was trapped in a nightmare of loneliness, degradation and violence, Jak had been 'saving money' he hadn't earned so that he could marry someone else and build the house he always told me we would live in together one day with our children. The thought of him living in 'our house' with his wife was almost worse than anything else.

I didn't ever see Jak again. The brief conversation I had with Vasos that day forced me to consider the possibility that he was an unscrupulous, self-serving, amoral criminal. But it wasn't until fairly recently that I finally stopped making excuses for him in my heart and accepted what he had done. One of the many difficult things I had to come to terms with was the fact that I had set out on what I had thought was going to be my life with Jak feeling like a hero. I had believed him when he told me that his mother was very ill and, in a way, I had been proud of myself for doing something in order to earn the money to pay for the operation that might save her life. Or maybe that was simply how I justified it to myself at the time, so that I didn't have to acknowledge the reality, which was that I was gullible, easily manipulated and too lacking in self-confidence to say no.

When understanding finally came, it sent my whole world crashing down around me. In some ways, I would have preferred never to have known the truth – at least then I would have been left with the illusion that someone really had loved me and cared about me.

When Mum and I flew home to England at the end of the week, we didn't stay with my grandparents, as the doctor at the hospital had wanted me to do, although we did meet up with them a few days after we got back. Nikos had insisted on giving Mum enough money to support us both until we could work out what to do next, and she had booked us into a bed and breakfast just around the corner from where some friends of hers lived.

Within a couple of days of arriving back in England, she made an appointment for me to see a doctor. I didn't tell him anything about what I had been doing in Greece; I just said I had been depressed and I showed him the tablets I'd been given by the psychiatrist. He looked at the labels on the bottles carefully, then scooped them all up and dumped them in the bin beside his desk. 'Just take these,' he said, handing me a prescription for the anti-depressant Prozac.

When we left the doctor's surgery, Mum took me to a pharmacy to get the new tablets and then to a walk-in sexual health clinic. I hated having to contaminate my new life by admitting I'd had syphilis. I told the nurse that I had been treated for it in Greece and she said it would be a good idea to do some tests to make sure everything was okay. I knew I hadn't taken the tablets exactly the way I should have done, but I was shocked when she said I still had it.

'We can clear it up now with an injection of penicillin,' she said, in a matter-of-fact, non-judgemental way that made me feel grateful to her. 'It hurts a bit – we do it in your backside – but the good news is that you only need to have one.'

I hate injections, and now that no one was hurting me on an almost daily basis, I hated the thought of being hurt. I must have looked as miserable as I felt, because the nurse touched my arm and said, 'You do need to get rid of it, Megan. I expect you've looked on the internet, so you'll know what the long-term effects can be if it isn't cleared up completely.'

In fact, I hadn't looked it up at all. At the time, the prospect of having to do anything about anything was overwhelmingly daunting. As far as the syphilis was concerned, I think I had hoped that if I ignored it, it might go away. I knew that was stupid though. So I gritted my teeth and had the injection.

The nurse was right about it hurting, but when she had done it she said, 'You're the first person I've ever known who didn't even flinch.' What she didn't know, of course, was that I'd had an almost infinite number of far more painful experiences, as well as lots of practice at detaching my mind when horrible things were being done to my body.

Even now, only fear and sudden loud noises make me flinch. For example, after I had been back in England for a few months, I was standing at some pedestrian lights in the town centre, waiting to cross the road, when two men came up behind me. They were talking quite loudly, joking with each other, and when one of them raised his arm I cringed and took a sideways step away from him. The man laughed and said, 'Bloody hell, love! What's up with you? You don't have to cower away from me like that. I'm not going to bite you or murder you or something.' So I laughed too and made a joke of it.

I'm still afraid of strangers. I used to tell myself, 'You're all right now. You're safe. You don't have to worry about anything.' But I could never quite make myself believe it.

After Mum went back to Greece, I began the task of trying to rebuild my life, and found myself struggling in all sorts of ways. If you don't have any self-respect, it's difficult to do the sort of things 'self-respecting people' do – like apply for jobs or believe you have a right to be treated decently. I did have a few low-paid jobs and I worked in a shop for a while, but for someone who jumped at every sound and viewed every male customer with anxious suspicion, it wasn't surprising that I didn't last very long.

As the weeks passed and I became better able to control my instinctive overreaction to strangers, I got another job working in a shop, where I became friendly with another girl who worked there called Claire. When I got to know her, I told her a bit about my story and said that I was scared because I thought people connected to the traffickers might be looking for me in England.

I think Claire must have said something to the owner of the shop, because one day, just before closing time, a man came in and started talking to me, asking me about myself. I was nervous at first, and even thought for a moment that it might be some sort of trap. But the man was pleasant and not in any way intimidating, and when he told me that he worked for an anti-trafficking charity and gave me a phone number to call if I ever needed someone to talk to, I took the bit of paper he held out to me.

I didn't call the number immediately. In fact, I almost forgot about it, until I got fed up with walking down roads with my fists clenched, trying to stop myself turning round to see if anyone really was following me. Within days of plucking up the courage to make that phone call, I was in a safe house in London.

After all the turmoil and chaos I had been used to, it was like living in a calm, well-organised family home. The people who ran the safe house were supportive and taught me some of the life skills I had missed out on learning during my lost teenage years. I still had terrible nightmares, many of which involved the sound of gunshots, and I would often wake up sobbing, convinced that Christoph was standing in the shadows of the bedroom. What had changed, though, was that now when I woke up in the night, sweating and frightened, I could go downstairs and there would be someone to talk to and to tell me everything was all right and I was safe.

There were three other girls in the house while I was there. They had all been trafficked and one of them had a baby. You might assume we would have talked to each other about what had happened to us, but we didn't really say much at all. Perhaps we didn't need to. I think there was a silently acknowledged bond between us, which would certainly explain why none of the other girls told the staff when I started drinking again. I was breaking one of the strictest rules of the house, and this time there really was no one else to blame but myself.

I told myself that drinking was just a coping mechanism. But I had seen the damage alcohol can do and I should have known better than anyone that it doesn't help you to cope at all; quite the reverse, in fact.

I managed to keep it a secret for a while, until I got really drunk one day and started crying and carrying on downstairs. The staff at the house must have realised immediately what was wrong with me. When they searched my room and found the bottle, they called an ambulance and I was taken to hospital and sectioned. I had been in the safe house for about six months and I thought at the time that it was rather a drastic overreaction to my getting drunk, but I think they were scared – for me, for the other very vulnerable girls in the house and for the baby. Maybe they hoped, too, that it would be a wake-up call that would make me realise wrong decisions have consequences. It was certainly a shock to find myself in a psychiatric hospital again.

When I was discharged from the hospital after just a few days, they wouldn't let me go back to the safe house: I had broken the rules and there were no second chances. I was devastated. Just when I was finally getting the practical and emotional support I so desperately needed, I had messed it all up. A voice in my head kept saying, 'Stupid. Stupid. Stupid.' What made me feel even worse was the knowledge that I had let down the people who had trusted me and who had done everything they could to try to help me.

Fortunately, with the help and support of my grandparents, I was eventually able to move into a small rented flat. Then I found a part-time job and enrolled on a course at college to try to catch up on my prematurely terminated education. I still find it difficult to stick at things, and sometimes it all feels too difficult and too much of struggle. When that happens, I remind myself that at least I now have a future, which, for a long time, is something I didn't think I would ever have.

I'm determined not to see myself as a victim. I used to get frustrated and miserable because I didn't seem to be getting over what happened to me in Greece – until I realised that I wasn't ever going to 'get over' it. That doesn't mean I'm constantly replaying the events of those years in my mind. I know that I have to accept the fact that, as I can't change what happened, I need to focus my energies on keeping it in the past and learning to live with it. I used to blame myself for everything, but I know now that, at 14 years old, I wasn't really responsible for it, or emotionally strong enough to resist it.

Some people will blame me entirely for everything that happened to me and perhaps particularly for not attempting to escape when I had the opportunity to do so. Someone told me recently that hostages and kidnap victims can develop something called Stockholm syndrome, which makes them empathise with their captors and even form strong attachments with them. I think the idea is that affected hostages respond defensively to the trauma of being threatened and beaten by starting to see *lack* of abuse as kindness. Maybe that's what happened to me. The reasons don't really matter now.

I don't blame my mum for it either: I know she'll always regret leaving me with Jak. Mum and Nikos are still together. They've moved away from the town where they met – and where I met Jak – but they've stayed in Greece. I'll never go back to Greece, so I really miss her. We talk regularly on the phone and she comes to England as often as she can, and I've got my grandparents, who would do whatever they could to help me if I ever needed it. Old habits die hard though, and I still have a tendency to pretend that everything's okay, even when it isn't.

I'm lucky to have had the support of some really good friends, and particularly of my sister. I didn't see or have any contact with my sister for six years, so I'm really grateful to have a good relationship with her now. She's doing really well and I'm very proud of her. I haven't said much about her in my story because I don't want to drag her into it. As things turned out, not coming to Greece with Mum and me was probably the best thing that could have happened to her.

It's funny: when I was in Greece I was worried about not having a future; now that I'm back here, it's the past that's at the root of all my problems. All I can do is try to focus on making the best of whatever lies ahead. It isn't easy; I often feel as though I'm struggling to keep my head above water while swimming round and round in a pool of black despair. Sometimes, the anger that is always there in a tight little knot inside me bursts out and I fly into a rage. I've never physically hurt anyone though, other than myself. For a while, whenever it all got too much, I would get drunk; then the fear would come back and I would start to cry. But mostly I do what everyone else does: I cope the best way I can.

I didn't even know human trafficking existed when I went to Greece at the age of 14. In fact, I was just one of an estimated 2.4 million men, women and children who are currently victims of human trafficking around the world. Some of them are physically incarcerated, while others are imprisoned – as I was – by fear, threats and violence. The buying and selling of people is big business, which generates a massive global income second only to that of drug trafficking.

I want to tell you that since I've been back in England I've moved on and I'm doing great. The truth is that I haven't and I'm not. But I *am* doing okay, and I know things will get better. There are always going to be times when my life stalls and when even treading water seems to require a huge amount of effort I simply can't make. That's just the way it is. I can't change it, so I have to learn to live with it. I'm not going to let it beat me though. For almost six years from the age of 14, I lived a life of unrelenting isolation, degradation and brutality. If I can survive that – and I did – I know that I can survive anything.

What happened to me in Greece will affect me for the rest of my life – both mentally and physically, in the form of the injuries I sustained during the course of many beatings. I still battle against low self-esteem and I often have nightmares that are so real and terrifying that I'm afraid to go back to sleep. But I know now that I was one of the lucky ones, because I escaped and I *do* have a future; whereas many of the other millions of people who are currently victims of trafficking will continue to be bought and sold for the rest of their lives.

Some Facts about Modern-day Slavery

Every day, in countries throughout the world, countless numbers of men, women and children are being forced to work long hours, often in appalling conditions for little or no pay. Most of them will never be rescued or see their homes or loved ones again.

It is difficult to estimate accurately the number of people who are currently being exploited for forced labour worldwide. Some research indicates that the figure is 20.9 million. Other reports put it even higher, at 30 million, including 5.5 million children.

Not all victims of exploitation are trafficked across borders and to other countries. According to a report by the UN Office on Drugs and Crime, there were 2.4 million victims of human trafficking worldwide in 2012, 80 per cent of whom were being exploited as sexual slaves. But, again, other research indicates that the true figure is much higher, at around 9 million.

Globalisation and the demand for cheap labour have helped to make modern-day slavery a lucrative business. The income earned by the criminals who buy and sell other human beings is estimated to be a massive $150 billion a year – an amount that is almost exactly equal to the entire UK budget for the NHS in the year 2013/14.

In 2008, 42 countries had signed and ratified the Council of Europe Convention on Action against Trafficking in Human Beings. When the Convention came into force in the UK the following year, this country became bound by its rules and the National Referral Mechanism (NRM) was set in motion.

The role of the NRM is to identify victims of human trafficking who have been trafficked into, out of or within the UK, and provide them with support and protection. It also collects and passes on information to the UK Human Trafficking Centre for the purpose of gaining a better understanding of the extent and scope of the problem.

In 2013, the NRM received 1,746 referrals of potential victims of trafficking from 112 countries. First on the list was Albania, with 268 referrals; then Nigeria with 186; Vietnam with 181; Romania with 104; and, in fifth place, the UK with 90. Trafficking victims can be referred to the NRM by numerous agencies – including the police, the Home Office, the Salvation Army and other charitable organisations – but only with their consent. As a result, these figures are a significant underestimate of the real situation in the UK – a fact that has become shockingly apparent following recent horrific reports of the sexual abuse of children and young people in Rotherham and Rochdale. The truth is that we can only imagine how many men, women and children in this country are living lives of abject misery while being subjected to ruthless exploitation.

There are many reasons why people are vulnerable to slavery. Some victims are incredibly poor and have been offered jobs they thought would lift their families out of poverty. Some have put their trust in untrustworthy people and have been tricked by boyfriends, family friends or other people who appeared to care about them. And some have been displaced as refugees or left widowed or orphaned by war. Whatever their circumstances and whatever country they came from or were trafficked to, the one common thread that unites them all is that each and every one of them is somebody's brother, sister, son, daughter, mother, father, husband, wife, nephew, niece or friend.

It's important to be aware of the facts and figures related to modern-day slavery. But it's even more important to remember that behind the statistics there are human beings who deserve, as we all do, the most basic human right of being able to live their lives in peace and freedom.

A Police Perspective on Human Trafficking in the UK

by Robin*

As a Detective Constable working for a UK Sexual Crime Unit, I've seen a massive change during the last 12 months in terms of the commitment of all agencies involved in tackling human trafficking. We now work a lot more closely with the NHS and local authorities, as well as alongside the Home Office Border Force in an attempt to identify victims of human trafficking as they pass through airports. My own police force is also in the process of training every frontline police officer and police community support officer (PCSO) to identify and assist possible victims.

* Robin (not his real name) played a vital role in protecting and supporting trafficking victim Sophie Hayes (author of the book *Trafficked*) when she was pursued in England by the man who had trafficked her to Italy.

Perhaps as a direct result of this increased awareness, something else that has changed in recent months is the way traffickers operate. For example, many victims of sex trafficking are now being taken to hotels, rather than to the more stereotypical 'massage parlour' brothels. The traffickers advertise on certain websites, take bookings for three or four days and then move on to another hotel in another area. Other victims are being held in houses in residential streets, where they live and are visited by clients, rather than being moved about as they would have been in the past.

Labour trafficking has also increased in the last few years – or, at least, it is being reported more often. But we are still a long way from establishing the true extent of the problem in the UK. One of the reasons for that is the fact that many victims of labour trafficking don't really understand that they are being exploited. For example, what often happens is that someone living in abject poverty in an Eastern European country is promised a reasonably paid job in the UK. Then, when they get here, they are paid just a few pounds a day and have to sleep in a small room with five other men in the same situation. They may feel they don't have any choice – maybe they've entered the country illegally or owe the traffickers money for bringing them here – and they tell themselves that at least they're earning a couple of pounds more than they would be getting at home.

There are many different types of labour trafficking and exploitation occurring in the UK today: young Vietnamese males forced to stay in buildings that are being used as cannabis farms to tend the plants; Vietnamese females working in nail bars for next to no money; males and females of all nationalities picking vegetables; and males working on fishing vessels who don't set foot on dry land for months on end and who, again, earn little or no money.

The police and the general public in this country have a greater awareness of trafficking and slavery than they did just a short time ago. But we are still nowhere near rescuing enough victims. To be able to make a real impact, the police need the help and support of the public – just as they do when tackling any sort of crime. We need people to be nosy about the local car wash or nail bar and about the house on their street that is visited by men at all hours of the day and night and lived in by women who rarely go out. The following are some of the possible indicators to look out for:

- Do people appear to be living and working at the same address?
- Are they collected very early in the morning and/or returned late at night on a regular basis?
- Do they have inappropriate clothing for the work they are performing and/or lack safety equipment?
- Do they have any signs of physical injury or malnourishment?
- Do they look unkempt?

- Are they isolated from the local community and/or appear to be under the control or influence of others?

It is important, too, that victims of trafficking themselves understand that the police in the UK *want* to help them. There aren't the issues of corruption here that there might be amongst the police forces in their own countries and they need to know they can trust us. Despite what the traffickers may tell them, if they are genuine victims of trafficking, there will probably be no immigration issues involved in our dealings with them. The same goes for British nationals who have been trafficked within the UK or abroad: whatever the circumstances, they can come to the police for help and support. Or, if they don't feel they can go to the police for some reason, they can contact Crime Stoppers or the Modern Slavery helpline.

Crime Stoppers

Phone number: 0800 555 111
Website: https://crimestoppers-uk.org

Modern Slavery

Phone number: 0800 0121 700
Website: https://modernslavery.co.uk

Also available

The story of how a British girl was forced into the dark and dangerous world of the sex trade – and how she survived.

Moving Memoirs

Stories of hope, courage and the power of love…

If you loved this book, then you will love our Moving Memoirs eNewsletter

Sign up to…

- Be the first to hear about new books

- Get sneak previews from your favourite authors

- Read exclusive interviews

- Be entered into our monthly prize draw to win one of our latest releases before it's even hit the shops!

Sign up at

www.moving-memoirs.com